maranGraphics'™
Simplified Computer Guide
Microsoft® Excel 4.0 for Windows™

Ruth Maran

maranGraphics Inc.
Mississauga, Ontario, Canada

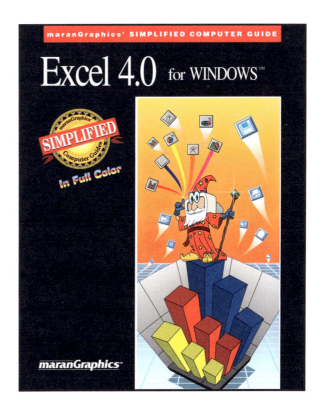

maranGraphics'™ Simplified Computer Guide
Microsoft ® Excel 4.0 for Windows™

Copyright©   maranGraphics Inc., 1992
5755 Coopers Avenue
Mississauga, Ontario, Canada
L4Z 1R9
Telephone: (416) 890-3300
Fax: (416) 890-9434

Screen shots ©1987-1991 Microsoft Corporation. Reprinted with permission from Microsoft Corporation.

Published 1992.

Canadian Cataloguing in Publication Data

Maran, Ruth
    MaranGraphics' simplified computer guide,
Microsoft Excel 4.0 for Windows

Includes index.

1. Microsoft Excel (Computer program). 2. Microsoft Excel 4 for Windows. 3. Business - Computer programs. 4. WINDOWS (Computer program). I. Title.

HF5548.4.M523M52 1992   650'.0285'5369   C92-094769-7

All rights reserved. No part of this publication may be used, reproduced or transmitted, in any form or by any means, electronic, mechanical, photocopying, recording or otherwise, or stored in any retrieval system of any nature, without the prior written permission of the copyright holder, application for which shall be made to: maranGraphics Inc., 5755 Coopers Avenue, Mississauga, Ontario, Canada, L4Z 1R9.

This publication is sold with the understanding that neither maranGraphics Inc., nor its dealers or distributors, warrants the contents of the publication, either expressly or impliedly, and, without limiting the generality of the foregoing, no warranty either express or implied is made regarding this publication's quality, performance, salability, capacity, suitability or fitness with respect to any specific or general function, purpose or application. Neither maranGraphics Inc., nor its dealers or distributors shall be liable to the purchaser or any other person or entity in any shape, manner or form whatsoever regarding liability, loss or damage caused or alleged to be caused directly or indirectly by this publication.

Acknowledgements

Special thanks to Victor Pitchkur of Microsoft Canada Inc., and to Saverio C. Tropiano, B.Sc., B.A. for their support and consultation.

To the dedicated staff at maranGraphics Inc. and HyperImage Inc., including Monica DeVries, Jim C. Leung, Jill Maran, Judy Maran, Robert Maran, David Ross and Gavin Yong for their contributions.

To Eric Feistmantl who was always there to solve my technical and operational problems.

To Maxine Maran for providing the organizational skill to keep the project under control.

And finally, a special appreciation to Richard Maran who originated the easy-to-use graphic format of this guide. Thank you for your inspiration and guidance.

Trademark Acknowledgements

Microsoft, MS and MS-DOS, are registered trademarks of Microsoft Corporation.

Autosum, the Microsoft Mouse design, and Windows are trademarks of Microsoft Corporation.

HP, Hewlett-Packard, LaserJet and DeskJet are registered trademarks of Hewlett-Packard Company.

Q+E is a trademark of Pioneer Software Systems Corporation.

Cover Design & Graphics Consultant:
Jim C. Leung

Art Director:
Jim C. Leung

Production:
Monica DeVries
Jim C. Leung
David Ross

Linotronic L-330 Output:
HyperImage Inc.

Table of Contents

	Page
READ ME FIRST	2

GETTING STARTED
Start Microsoft Excel 4
Maximize and Restore a Window 6
Exit Microsoft Excel 6
Help 8
Select Cells 10
Moving Through a Worksheet 12

ENTER DATA
Enter Text 14
Enter Numbers 14
Edit Data 16
Undo 16
AutoFill Text 18
AutoFill the Same Data 18
AutoFill Numbers 20
Delete Data 20

ENTER FORMULAS AND FUNCTIONS
Introduction to Formulas 22
Enter Formulas 24
AutoFill Formulas 24
Introduction to Functions 26
Enter Functions 28
Sum Using the AutoSum Tool 28
AutoFill Functions 30
Absolute References 30

MANAGING YOUR FILES
Files and Directories 32
Save a Worksheet 34-36
Close a Worksheet 36
Open a Saved Worksheet 38
Create a New Worksheet 38
Switch Between Worksheets 39
Arrange Worksheets 40
Delete a Worksheet 40

EDIT A WORKSHEET
Change Column Width 42
Change Row Height 44
Insert or Delete a Row 46
Insert or Delete a Column 47
Move or Copy Data 48-50

FORMAT A WORKSHEET
Display or Hide a Toolbar 52
Format Numbers 52
Change Fonts 54
Align Data 56
Borders and Shading 58
Remove Formats 59
Copy and Paste Formats 60
Bold, Italic, and Underline 60
AutoFormat 62
The Drawing Toolbar 64

CREATE AND EDIT A CHART
Create a Chart 66-68
Move a Chart 70
Change Chart Data 70
Resize a Chart 71
Change Chart Type or Format 72
Rotate a Chart 74

PRINT
Change Page Setup 76
Preview a Worksheet 78
Print a Worksheet 80

OUTLINE A WORKSHEET
Display the Utility Toolbar 82
Create an Outline 82
Collapse a Level 84
Expand a Level 84
Hide an Outline 85

CREATE AND USE A DATABASE
Create a Database 86
Sort a Database 86
Display the Data Form 88
Find a Record 88
Add a Record 89
Change a Record 90
Delete a Record 90
Extract Records 92

INDEX 94

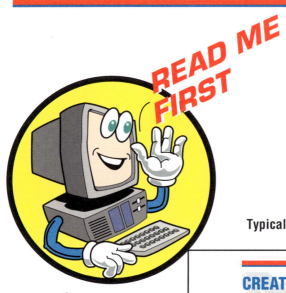

READ ME FIRST

Microsoft® Excel 4.0 for Windows™ is a spreadsheet package used to create documents that help you organize, analyze, and perform calculations on your data.

maranGraphics uses a unique two-page format, as illustrated to the right.

The screen-by-screen method displays exactly what you see on screen as you move through the program.

All chapters in this guide are listed on the right side of each two-page format. The current chapter is highlighted in red type.

All topics within the current chapter are displayed on the top right of each two-page format. The current topic is highlighted in red type.

Think of it as being in a shopping mall, using a "You Are Here" display to find a particular store.

Typical Two-Page Format

CREATE A CHART

The ChartWizard leads you through five steps to create a chart using data from your worksheet.

In this example, the Revenue and Total Expenses for the months of Jan, Feb, and Mar will be charted.

Data Range to be Charted (Step 1 of 5)

1 Select the column headings you want to chart (example: **A3** to **D3**).

2 Press and hold down the **Ctrl** key as you select the other rows you want to chart (example: **A5** to **D5**, then **A10** to **D10**).

3 Release the mouse button, then the **Ctrl** key.

4 Click the **ChartWizard** tool and the mouse pointer changes to +.

Chart Type (Step 2 of 5)

1 Click the desired chart type (example: **3-D Column**).

2 Click the **Next** button to move to **Step 3** of the **ChartWizard**.

START MICROSOFT EXCEL

  Start Microsoft Excel

1 To start Microsoft® Excel from MS-DOS, type **win**. Then press **Enter**.

■ The **Program Manager** window is displayed.

All your programs (example: **Word for Windows 2.0**, **Microsoft Excel 4.0**) are started from the Program Manager.

2 To open the **Microsoft Excel 4.0** group icon, move the mouse pointer over its icon and click the left button twice in quick succession.

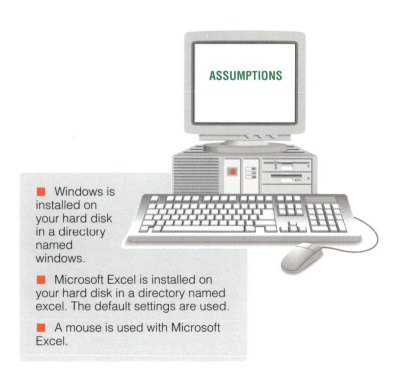

ASSUMPTIONS

■ Windows is installed on your hard disk in a directory named windows.

■ Microsoft Excel is installed on your hard disk in a directory named excel. The default settings are used.

■ A mouse is used with Microsoft Excel.

4

| START MICROSOFT EXCEL | MAXIMIZE AND RESTORE A WINDOW | EXIT MICROSOFT EXCEL | HELP | SELECT CELLS | MOVING THROUGH A WORKSHEET |

GETTING STARTED

- ENTER DATA
- ENTER FORMULAS AND FUNCTIONS
- MANAGING YOUR FILES
- EDIT A WORKSHEET
- FORMAT A WORKSHEET
- CREATE AND EDIT A CHART
- PRINT
- OUTLINE A WORKSHEET
- CREATE AND USE A DATABASE

- The **Microsoft Excel 4.0** group window appears.

3 To start the **Microsoft Excel** program, move the mouse pointer over its icon and click the left button twice in quick succession.

- Microsoft Excel opens up a new worksheet called **Sheet1**.

- This worksheet window is also called a document. The name of the document can be renamed when you save it to your hard disk.

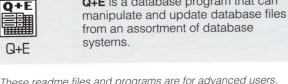

The **readme.txt** file contains the latest revisions and notes for Microsoft Excel.

The **network.txt** file contains information on using Microsoft Excel in a network environment.

The **Dialog Editor** is used to create custom dialog boxes for macros.

Q+E is a database program that can manipulate and update database files from an assortment of database systems.

Note: These readme files and programs are for advanced users. Refer to your Microsoft Excel User's Guide for more information.

 USING THE KEYBOARD

If key names are separated by a plus sign (+), press and hold down the first key before pressing the second key (example: **Shift**+**Tab**).

If key names are separated by a comma (,), press and release the first key before pressing the second key (example: **Alt**,**F**).

USING THE MOUSE

For this guide, the following shortcuts are used:

- "Move the mouse pointer over **xx** and click the left button" becomes:

  Click xx

- "Move the mouse pointer over **xx** and click the left button twice in quick succession" becomes:

  Double click xx

5

MAXIMIZE AND RESTORE A WINDOW

EXIT MICROSOFT EXCEL

Maximize a Window

A worksheet can be enlarged to view a larger working area.

1 Click the **Sheet1** window's **Maximize** button.

■ The **Sheet1** window is enlarged to fill the entire workspace.

Restore a Window

2 Click the **Sheet1** window's **Restore** button.

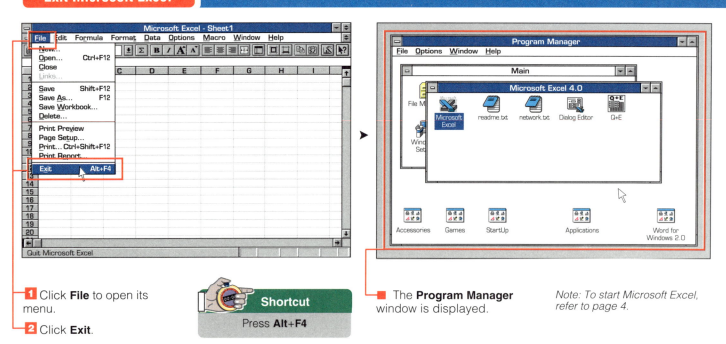

Exit Microsoft Excel

1 Click **File** to open its menu.

2 Click **Exit**.

Shortcut
Press **Alt+F4**

■ The **Program Manager** window is displayed.

Note: To start Microsoft Excel, refer to page 4.

| START MICROSOFT EXCEL | **MAXIMIZE AND RESTORE A WINDOW** | **EXIT MICROSOFT EXCEL** | HELP | SELECT CELLS | MOVING THROUGH A WORKSHEET |

GETTING STARTED

- ENTER DATA
- ENTER FORMULAS AND FUNCTIONS
- MANAGING YOUR FILES
- EDIT A WORKSHEET
- FORMAT A WORKSHEET
- CREATE AND EDIT A CHART
- PRINT
- OUTLINE A WORKSHEET
- CREATE AND USE A DATABASE

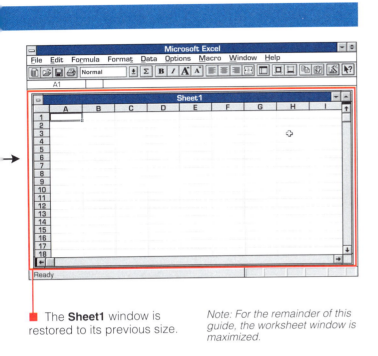

■ The **Sheet1** window is restored to its previous size.

Note: For the remainder of this guide, the worksheet window is maximized.

KEYBOARD SHORTCUT TO SELECT MENU COMMANDS

■ To select a menu command (example: **Exit**), press **Alt**,**F**,**X**.

F is the underlined letter for the **F**ile menu.

X is the underlined letter for the E**x**it command.

*Note: Microsoft Excel commands are not case sensitive. You can press **Alt**,**F**,**X** or **Alt**,**f**,**x**.*

*If a dimmed command appears, this means it is not currently operational (example: **Links**).*

■ Some commands display alternative keyboard shortcuts. For example, to select the **Exit** command, press **Alt+F4**.

If this dialog box appears when trying to exit Microsoft Excel, you have not saved changes you made to the worksheet.

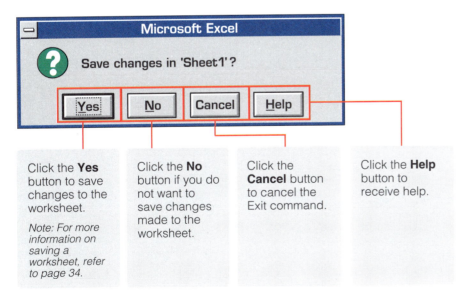

Click the **Yes** button to save changes to the worksheet.

Note: For more information on saving a worksheet, refer to page 34.

Click the **No** button if you do not want to save changes made to the worksheet.

Click the **Cancel** button to cancel the Exit command.

Click the **Help** button to receive help.

7

HELP

Context Sensitive Help

This feature permits you to receive help information for any item on the screen by clicking that item.

1 Click the **Help** tool and the mouse pointer changes to.

2 To receive help on a menu command, click a menu title (example: **File**) to open its menu.

■ The File menu is opened.

3 Click the command (example: **Exit**) you want help on.

Help Contents

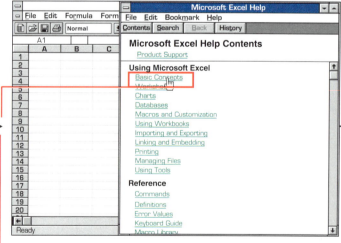

Help Contents displays a list of the main Help topics.

1 Click **Help** to open its menu.

2 Click **Contents** and the **Microsoft Excel Help** window appears.

3 Move the mouse pointer over a topic you want information on (example: **Basic Concepts**), and it turns into. Then click the left mouse button.

Note: This only applies to underlined text.

8

| START MICROSOFT EXCEL | MAXIMIZE AND RESTORE A WINDOW | EXIT MICROSOFT EXCEL | **HELP** | SELECT CELLS | MOVING THROUGH A WORKSHEET |

GETTING STARTED

- ENTER DATA
- ENTER FORMULAS AND FUNCTIONS
- MANAGING YOUR FILES
- EDIT A WORKSHEET
- FORMAT A WORKSHEET
- CREATE AND EDIT A CHART
- PRINT
- OUTLINE A WORKSHEET
- CREATE AND USE A DATABASE

■ The **Microsoft Excel Help** window appears.

4 Move the mouse pointer over a term you want information on (example: **Clipboard**) and it turns into 👆. Then click the left mouse button.

Note: This only applies to dotted, underlined text.

■ A detailed explanation of that term appears.

5 Click anywhere on the screen to remove the explanation.

6 To exit **Microsoft Excel Help**, double click its Control menu box ▭.

■ A detailed explanation of that topic appears.

4 Move the mouse pointer over the next topic of interest and it turns into 👆. Then click the left mouse button.

5 To exit **Microsoft Excel Help**, double click its Control menu box ▭.

ADDITIONAL CHOICES

Contents — Click this button to view a list of the main Help topics.

Search — Click this button to search for information on a specific word or phrase.

Back — Click this button to return to the last topic you displayed.

History — Click this button to view a list of the last topics you displayed. Then double click the topic you want to view again.

9

SELECT CELLS

Select a Cell

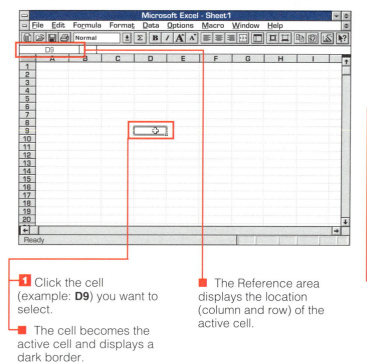

1 Click the cell (example: **D9**) you want to select.

■ The cell becomes the active cell and displays a dark border.

■ The Reference area displays the location (column and row) of the active cell.

Select a Row

1 To select a row, click the row heading (example: **5**).

Note: To cancel the selection, click anywhere on the worksheet.

Select a Cell Range

1 Move the mouse pointer ✥ over the first cell of the range (example: **B3**) you want to select.

2 Click and hold down the left mouse button.

3 Still holding down the button, drag the mouse to select the cell range.

4 Release the mouse button.

Note: To cancel the selection, click anywhere on the worksheet.

| START MICROSOFT EXCEL | MAXIMIZE AND RESTORE A WINDOW | EXIT MICROSOFT EXCEL | HELP | **SELECT CELLS** | MOVING THROUGH A WORKSHEET |

Select a Column

1 To select a column, click the column heading (example: **F**).

Note: To cancel the selection, click anywhere on the worksheet.

Select the Entire Worksheet

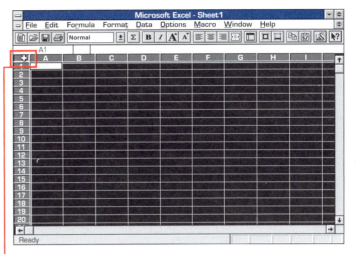

1 To select the entire worksheet, click the **Select All** button.

Note: To cancel the selection, click anywhere on the worksheet.

Select Two Cell Ranges

5 To select a second range of cells, move the mouse pointer ✛ over the first cell of the range (example: **E9**) you want to select.

6 Press and hold down the **Ctrl** key.

7 Still holding down the **Ctrl** key, drag the mouse to select the second cell range.

8 Release the **Ctrl** key, then release the mouse button.

*Note: To select more than two cell ranges, repeat steps **5** to **8**.*

IMPORTANT

You must select the cells you want to work with before executing most Microsoft Excel commands.

GETTING STARTED

- ENTER DATA
- ENTER FORMULAS AND FUNCTIONS
- MANAGING YOUR FILES
- EDIT A WORKSHEET
- FORMAT A WORKSHEET
- CREATE AND EDIT A CHART
- PRINT
- OUTLINE A WORKSHEET
- CREATE AND USE A DATABASE

11

MOVING THROUGH A WORKSHEET

Using the Keyboard

MOVE ONE CELL IN ANY DIRECTION

Press ↑ to move one cell up.
Press ← to move one cell left.
Press ↓ to move one cell down.
Press → to move one cell right.

MOVE TO CELL A1

Press **Ctrl+Home** to move to cell **A1** from anywhere in the worksheet.

MOVE ONE SCREEN UP OR DOWN

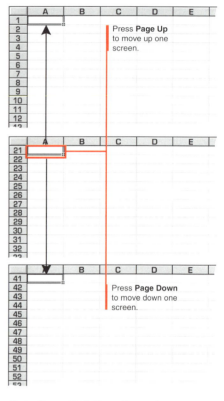

Press **Page Up** to move up one screen.

Press **Page Down** to move down one screen.

Note: Press **Ctrl+Page Down** to move one screen to the right. Press **Ctrl+Page Up** to move one screen to the left.

ACTION	KEYBOARD COMMAND
Move to the beginning of a row	Press **Home**
Move to the bottom edge of the worksheet (row 16384)	Press **Ctrl+** ↓ Note: If the worksheet contains data, these keys may have to be pressed more than once to get to the desired location.
Move to the right edge of the worksheet (column IV)	Press **Ctrl+** → Note: If the worksheet contains data, these keys may have to be pressed more than once to get to the desired location.
Move to the lower right corner of data stored in the worksheet	Press **Ctrl+End** Note: The worksheet must contain data for this to work.

NUM LOCK

■ To use the numeric keypad's arrows, PgUp, PgDn, Home and End keys, the **NUM** on the Status bar must be **off**.

If **NUM** on the Status bar is **on**, press [Num Lock] to turn it **off**.

| START MICROSOFT EXCEL | MAXIMIZE AND RESTORE A WINDOW | EXIT MICROSOFT EXCEL | HELP | SELECT CELLS | **MOVING THROUGH A WORKSHEET** |

 Using the Mouse

SCROLL UP OR DOWN

Scroll up one row

1 Click the **up arrow**.

Scroll down one row

1 Click the **down arrow**.

Scroll vertically to any position in the worksheet

1 Move the mouse pointer over the **Scroll box**. Click the left button and hold it down.

2 To move proportionally down the worksheet, drag the **Scroll box** proportionally (example: **halfway**) down the Scroll bar. Then release the button.

SCROLL LEFT OR RIGHT

Scroll left one column

1 Click the **left arrow**.

Scroll right one column

1 Click the **right arrow**.

Scroll horizontally to any position in the worksheet

1 Move the mouse pointer over the **Scroll box**. Click the left button and hold it down.

2 To move proportionally across the worksheet, drag the **Scroll box** proportionally (example: **halfway**) along the Scroll bar. Then release the button.

GETTING STARTED

- ENTER DATA
- ENTER FORMULAS AND FUNCTIONS
- MANAGING YOUR FILES
- EDIT A WORKSHEET
- FORMAT A WORKSHEET
- CREATE AND EDIT A CHART
- PRINT
- OUTLINE A WORKSHEET
- CREATE AND USE A DATABASE

13

ENTER TEXT

ENTER NUMBERS

Enter Text

1 Click the cell you want to enter text into (example: **B1**).

2 Type the text (example: **INCOME REPORT 1992**). As you type, the text appears in the active cell and in the formula bar.

*Note: If you make a mistake typing, press **Backspace** and retype.*

3 Click the Enter ✓ box, or press **Enter** to place the text in the cell.

*Note: To cancel the entry, click the Cancel ✗ box, or press **Esc**.*

■ The text is entered into the cell.

4 Click the next cell you want to enter text into (example: **A5**).

5 Type the text (example: **REVENUE**).

6 Click the Enter ✓ box, or press **Enter** to place the text in the cell.

*Note: To cancel the entry, click the Cancel ✗ box, or press **Esc**.*

Enter Numbers

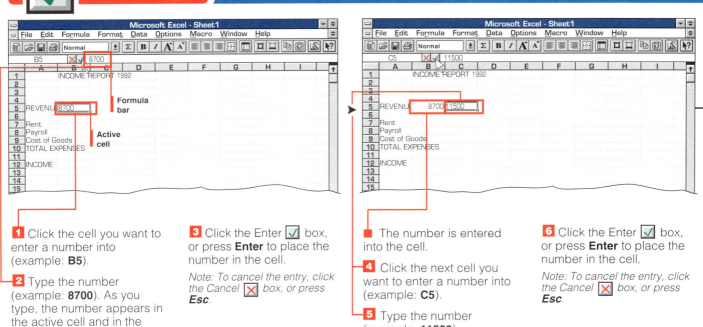

1 Click the cell you want to enter a number into (example: **B5**).

2 Type the number (example: **8700**). As you type, the number appears in the active cell and in the formula bar.

*Note: If you make a mistake typing, press **Backspace** and retype.*

3 Click the Enter ✓ box, or press **Enter** to place the number in the cell.

*Note: To cancel the entry, click the Cancel ✗ box, or press **Esc**.*

■ The number is entered into the cell.

4 Click the next cell you want to enter a number into (example: **C5**).

5 Type the number (example: **11500**).

6 Click the Enter ✓ box, or press **Enter** to place the number in the cell.

*Note: To cancel the entry, click the Cancel ✗ box, or press **Esc**.*

| ENTER TEXT | ENTER NUMBERS | EDIT DATA | UNDO | AUTOFILL TEXT | AUTOFILL THE SAME DATA | AUTOFILL NUMBERS | DELETE DATA |

GETTING STARTED

ENTER DATA

ENTER FORMULAS AND FUNCTIONS

MANAGING YOUR FILES

EDIT A WORKSHEET

FORMAT A WORKSHEET

CREATE AND EDIT A CHART

PRINT

OUTLINE A WORKSHEET

CREATE AND USE A DATABASE

■ The text is entered into the cell.

7 Type and enter the remaining text by repeating steps **1** to **3** for each text entry.

Shortcut
Press →, ←, ↓ or ↑ to enter text and move to the next cell.

LONG TEXT

■ If text is too long to fit in a cell, it spills over into the adjacent cell(s) if it is empty.

■ If the adjacent cell already contains data, Microsoft Excel displays as much of the text as the column width will allow. To display all text, the column must be widened (refer to page 42).

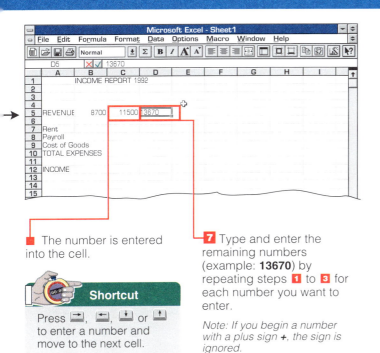

■ The number is entered into the cell.

7 Type and enter the remaining numbers (example: **13670**) by repeating steps **1** to **3** for each number you want to enter.

Note: If you begin a number with a plus sign +, the sign is ignored.

To enter a negative number, begin it with a minus sign – (example: –13670).

Shortcut
Press →, ←, ↓ or ↑ to enter a number and move to the next cell.

LONG NUMBERS

■ If a number is too long to fit in a cell, Microsoft Excel tries to display it exponentially.

■ If the exponential form is still too long, number signs (###) are displayed in the cell. To display the entire number, the column must be widened (refer to page 42).

15

EDIT DATA   UNDO

Edit Data

1 Click the cell that contains the data you want to change (example: **B1**).

2 In the formula bar, click and hold down the left mouse button as you drag over the character(s) you want to replace (example: **REPORT**). Then release the button.

3 Type the correction (example: **STATEMENT**).

*Note: If you make a mistake typing, press **Backspace** and retype.*

4 Click the Enter ✓ box, or press **Enter**.

Undo

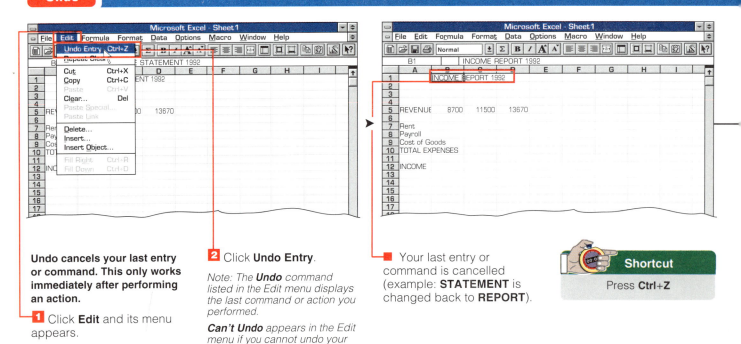

Undo cancels your last entry or command. This only works immediately after performing an action.

1 Click **Edit** and its menu appears.

2 Click **Undo Entry**.

*Note: The **Undo** command listed in the Edit menu displays the last command or action you performed.*

Can't Undo *appears in the Edit menu if you cannot undo your last action.*

■ Your last entry or command is cancelled (example: **STATEMENT** is changed back to **REPORT**).

Shortcut
Press **Ctrl+Z**

ENTER TEXT | ENTER NUMBERS | **EDIT DATA** | **UNDO** | AUTOFILL TEXT | AUTOFILL THE SAME DATA | AUTOFILL NUMBERS | DELETE DATA

GETTING STARTED

ENTER DATA

ENTER FORMULAS AND FUNCTIONS

MANAGING YOUR FILES

EDIT A WORKSHEET

FORMAT A WORKSHEET

CREATE AND EDIT A CHART

PRINT

OUTLINE A WORKSHEET

CREATE AND USE A DATABASE

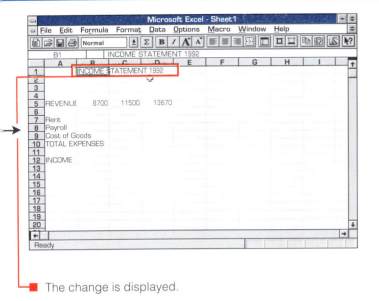

■ The change is displayed.

EDIT DATA USING THE KEYBOARD

1 Select the cell that contains the data you want to change.

2 Press **F2** to activate the formula bar.

3 Edit the entry by using the following keys:

Home	Move to the beginning of the data.
End	Move to the end of the data.
← or →	Move one character in the direction of the arrow.
Backspace	Delete the character to the left of the cursor.

3 To cancel the **Undo** command you just performed, click **Edit** to open its menu.

Note: This only works immediately after using the Undo command.

4 Click **Redo [u] Entry**.

Shortcut
Press **Ctrl+Z**

■ The last **Undo** command you performed is reversed (example: **REPORT** is changed back to **STATEMENT**).

17

AUTOFILL TEXT   AUTOFILL THE SAME DATA

➕ AutoFill Text

By using the AutoFill feature, Microsoft Excel can automatically enter a series into your worksheet. Examples are displayed below:

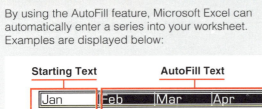

Starting Text	AutoFill Text		
Jan	Feb	Mar	Apr
Qtr 1	Qtr 2	Qtr 3	Qtr 4
Mon	Tue	Wed	Thu
Product 1	Product 2	Product 3	Product 4
2nd Term	3rd Term	4th Term	5th Term

Note: The AutoFill feature works in both the horizontal and vertical directions.

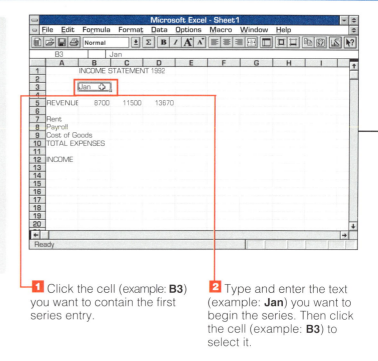

1 Click the cell (example: **B3**) you want to contain the first series entry.

2 Type and enter the text (example: **Jan**) you want to begin the series. Then click the cell (example: **B3**) to select it.

➕ AutoFill the Same Data

By using the AutoFill feature, Microsoft Excel can automatically copy the same data to all selected cells.

1 Click the cell (example: **B7**) you want to contain the data to be copied.

2 Type and enter the data (example: **1750**). Then click the cell (example: **B7**) to select it.

3 Move the mouse pointer ⇧ over the bottom right corner of the cell and it changes to ✚.

4 Click and hold down the left mouse button as you drag the pointer ✚ over the cells you want to AutoFill.

ENTER TEXT | ENTER NUMBERS | EDIT DATA | UNDO | **AUTOFILL TEXT** | **AUTOFILL THE SAME DATA** | AUTOFILL NUMBERS | DELETE DATA

GETTING STARTED

ENTER DATA

3 Move the mouse pointer ✥ over the bottom right corner of the cell (example: **B3**) and it changes to ✚.

4 Click and hold down the left mouse button as you drag the pointer ✚ over the cells you want to AutoFill.

5 Release the mouse button, and the series (example: **Feb**, **Mar**) is added to your worksheet.

ENTER FORMULAS AND FUNCTIONS

MANAGING YOUR FILES

EDIT A WORKSHEET

FORMAT A WORKSHEET

CREATE AND EDIT A CHART

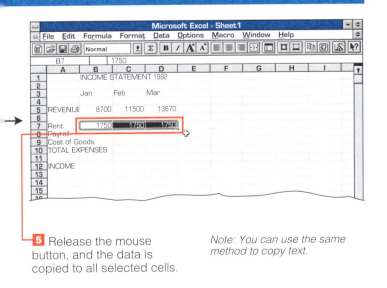

5 Release the mouse button, and the data is copied to all selected cells.

Note: You can use the same method to copy text.

PRINT

OUTLINE A WORKSHEET

CREATE AND USE A DATABASE

19

AUTOFILL NUMBERS / DELETE DATA

➕ AutoFill Numbers

By using the AutoFill feature, Microsoft Excel can automatically enter a series of numbers into your worksheet. Examples are displayed below:

Note: The AutoFill feature works in both the horizontal and vertical directions.

1 Click the cell (example: **G3**) you want to contain the first number of the series.

2 Type the number (example: **1**). Then press **Enter**.

Note: Payroll and Cost of Goods data was added to the worksheet.

3 Click the cell (example: **G4**) you want to contain the second number of the series.

4 Type the number (example: **2**). Then press **Enter**.

⌨ Delete Data

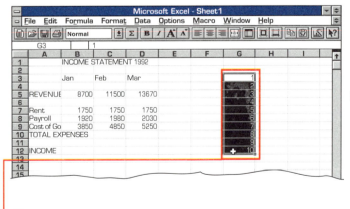

1 Select the cells you want to delete (example: **G3** to **G12**).

Note: To select cells, refer to page 10.

2 Press the **Delete** key and the **Clear** dialog box appears.

3 Click the **OK** button, or press **Enter**.

| ENTER TEXT | ENTER NUMBERS | EDIT DATA | UNDO | AUTOFILL TEXT | AUTOFILL THE SAME DATA | **AUTOFILL NUMBERS** | DELETE DATA |

5 Select the cells you want to begin the series (example: **G3** and **G4**).

Note: To select cells, refer to page 10.

6 Move the mouse pointer ⊕ over the bottom right corner of the selected cells and it changes to ✚.

7 Click and hold down the left mouse button as you drag the pointer ✚ over the cells you want to fill with the number series.

8 Release the mouse button and the number series is displayed.

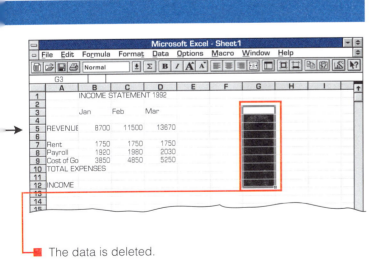

■ The data is deleted.

GETTING STARTED

- ENTER DATA
- ENTER FORMULAS AND FUNCTIONS
- MANAGING YOUR FILES
- EDIT A WORKSHEET
- FORMAT A WORKSHEET
- CREATE AND EDIT A CHART
- PRINT
- OUTLINE A WORKSHEET
- CREATE AND USE A DATABASE

21

INTRODUCTION TO FORMULAS

ORDER OF PRECEDENCE

■ Microsoft Excel performs operations in formulas based on the order of precedence.

■ Mathematical operators are included in formulas:

+   Add
*   Multiply
−   Subtract
/   Divide

OPERATION	ORDER OF PRECEDENCE
Multiplication 1 Division 1	Done in order of appearance
Addition 2 Subtraction 2	Done in order of appearance
Example:	15-3*4 is executed as follows: -3*4+15=3
Example:	18/2*3 is executed as follows: 18/2*3=27
Example:	1+2+3*4 is executed as follows: 3*4+1+2=15

OVERRIDING THE ORDER OF PRECEDENCE

To override the order of precedence, parentheses can be used:

Examples:

Formula	Execution
E5-E7*E9	15-3*4=3
(E5-E7)*E9	(15-3)*4=48
G5/H2*H7	18/2*3=27
G5/(H2*H7)	18/(2*3)=3
J5+J6+J7*J9	1+2+3*4=15
(J5+J6+J7)*J9	(1+2+3)*4=24

| INTRODUCTION TO FORMULAS | ENTER FORMULAS | AUTOFILL FORMULAS | INTRODUCTION TO FUNCTIONS | ENTER FUNCTIONS | SUM USING THE AUTOSUM TOOL | AUTOFILL FUNCTIONS | ABSOLUTE REFERENCES |

■ A formula performs calculations and contains mathematical operators, numbers and cell references.

■ Cell references are normally used in formulas instead of numbers. Then, if the numbers in the cells change, the formula automatically recalculates the new result.

■ The formula appears at the top of the screen when the cell containing the formula is active (example: **B11**).

■ A formula always starts with an equal sign **=**.

■ The result of the calculation appears in the cell containing the formula (example: **B11**).

■ **=B5+B6+B7-B9**

The cell reference B11 contains this formula.

If: B5=10
      B6=20
      B7=30
      B9=15

Then: The formula calculates 45.

B11=10+20+30-15=45

■ **=D5-D7*D9**

The cell reference D11 contains this formula.

If: D5=15
      D7=3
      D9=4

Then: The formula calculates 3.

D11=15-3*4=3

■ **=F5/G5*G7**

The cell reference G11 contains this formula.

If: F5=18
      G5=2
      G7=3

Then: The formula calculates 27.

G11=18/2*3=27

GETTING STARTED

ENTER DATA

ENTER FORMULAS AND FUNCTIONS

MANAGING YOUR FILES

EDIT A WORKSHEET

FORMAT A WORKSHEET

CREATE AND EDIT A CHART

PRINT

OUTLINE A WORKSHEET

CREATE AND USE A DATABASE

23

ENTER FORMULAS   AUTOFILL FORMULAS

Enter Formulas

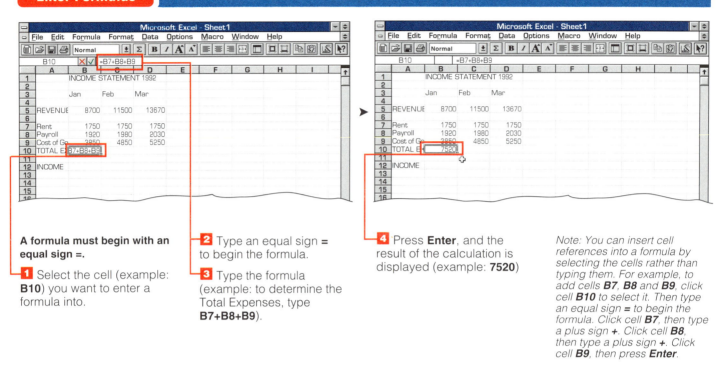

A formula must begin with an equal sign =.

1 Select the cell (example: **B10**) you want to enter a formula into.

2 Type an equal sign **=** to begin the formula.

3 Type the formula (example: to determine the Total Expenses, type **B7+B8+B9**).

4 Press **Enter**, and the result of the calculation is displayed (example: **7520**)

Note: You can insert cell references into a formula by selecting the cells rather than typing them. For example, to add cells **B7**, **B8** and **B9**, click cell **B10** to select it. Then type an equal sign **=** to begin the formula. Click cell **B7**, then type a plus sign **+**. Click cell **B8**, then type a plus sign **+**. Click cell **B9**, then press **Enter**.

AutoFill Formulas

By using the AutoFill feature, Microsoft Excel can automatically copy a formula to all selected cells.

1 Click the cell (example: **B10**) that contains the formula you want to copy to other cells.

2 Move the mouse pointer ⇧ over the bottom right corner of the cell and it changes to **+**.

3 Click and hold down the left mouse button as you drag the pointer **+** over the cells you want to copy the formula to.

24

| INTRODUCTION TO FORMULAS | ENTER FORMULAS | AUTOFILL FORMULAS | INTRODUCTION TO FUNCTIONS | ENTER FUNCTIONS | SUM USING THE AUTOSUM TOOL | AUTOFILL FUNCTIONS | ABSOLUTE REFERENCES |

Automatic Recalculation

Cell references are normally used in formulas instead of numbers. Then, if the numbers in the cells change, the formula automatically recalculates the new result.

1 Select the cell (example: **B8**) you want to edit.

2 Type the new number (example: **1890**).

3 Press **Enter**, and the formula recalculates the new result (example: **7490**).

4 Release the mouse button and the formula is copied to all selected cells.

5 Select a cell (example: **D10**) which received a copy of the formula.

■ Notice how the formula was adjusted and the result recalculated for that cell.

GETTING STARTED

ENTER DATA

ENTER FORMULAS AND FUNCTIONS

MANAGING YOUR FILES

EDIT A WORKSHEET

FORMAT A WORKSHEET

CREATE AND EDIT A CHART

PRINT

OUTLINE A WORKSHEET

CREATE AND USE A DATABASE

25

INTRODUCTION TO FUNCTIONS

■ Functions are formulas built into Microsoft Excel to perform time-saving set-up procedures.

■ Functions begin with the equal sign **=**.

■ The function name (example: **SUM**) can be typed in either upper or lower case, but spaces between characters are not allowed.

■ A function argument (example: **B6:B9**), enclosed in parentheses **( )**, specifies the data the function works on. Arguments can consist of numbers or cell references.

■ **=SUM(B6:B9)**

The cell reference B11 contains this function.

If: B6 = 2
     B7 = 1
     B8 = 3
     B9 = 5
Then: The function calculates 11.

B11=2+1+3+5=11

■ **=SUM(E6,E7,E9)**

The cell reference E11 contains this function.

If: E6 = 4
     E7 = 7
     E9 = 2
Then: The function calculates 13.

E11=4+7+2=13

■ **=AVERAGE(H6:H9)**

The cell reference H11 contains this function.

If: H6 = 3
     H7 = 6
     H8 = 2
     H9 = 1
Then: The function calculates 3.

H11=(3+6+2+1)/4=3

| INTRODUCTION TO FORMULAS | ENTER FORMULAS | AUTOFILL FORMULAS | **INTRODUCTION TO FUNCTIONS** | ENTER FUNCTIONS | SUM USING THE AUTOSUM TOOL | AUTOFILL FUNCTIONS | ABSOLUTE REFERENCES |

ARGUMENTS

■ An argument is a number or cell reference that tells Microsoft Excel the data you want the function to work on.

■ Arguments are always enclosed in parentheses ( ).

=SUM(A1,A2,A3,A4)

■ When you use a comma (,) between arguments, Microsoft Excel uses each number or cell reference when calculating the function.

For example: =SUM(A1,A2,A3,A4) is equal to =A1+A2+A3+A4

=SUM(A1:A4)

■ When you use a colon (:) between arguments, Microsoft Excel uses those two cell references plus all cell references in between them when calculating the function.

For example: =SUM(A1:A4) is equal to =SUM(A1,A2,A3,A4)

TYPICAL FUNCTIONS

SUM	Adds together the data in a list of values. Example: =SUM(C1:C9)	**MAX**	Finds the largest value in a list of values. Example: =MAX(B2:B70)
AVERAGE	Averages the data in a list of values. Example: =AVERAGE(B1:B6)	**MIN**	Finds the smallest value in a list of values. Example: =MIN(B2:B70)
DAYS360	Calculates the number of days between two dates. Example: =DAYS360("8/1/92","8/15/92") =14	**MEDIAN**	Finds the middle value in a list of values. Example: =MEDIAN(B2:B70)

Note: For a complete list of Functions, refer to the Microsoft Excel Function Reference guide.

GETTING STARTED

ENTER DATA

ENTER FORMULAS AND FUNCTIONS

MANAGING YOUR FILES

EDIT A WORKSHEET

FORMAT A WORKSHEET

CREATE AND EDIT A CHART

PRINT

OUTLINE A WORKSHEET

CREATE AND USE A DATABASE

ENTER FUNCTIONS

SUM USING THE AUTOSUM TOOL

Enter Functions

In the following example, the SUM function will be used to determine the total revenue.

*Note: The **Year-to-Date** column heading was entered into cell **E3**.*

1 Select the cell (example: E5) you want to enter the function into.

2 Type an equal sign **=** to begin the function.

3 Type the function name (example: **SUM**). Then type an open parenthesis **(**.

4 Click and hold down the left mouse button as you drag over the cells containing the numbers you want the function to work on (example: **B5** to **D5**). A dotted line appears around the selected cells.

5 Release the mouse button and the selected cells (example: **B5:D5**) are displayed in the formula bar.

*Note: You can also use the keyboard to specify which cells you want the function to work on (example: type **B5:D5**). For more information on arguments, refer to page 27.*

 ## Sum Using the AutoSum Tool

The AutoSum tool can quickly add a single row or column of data.

1 Click the cell (example: E7) you want to display the result of the added data.

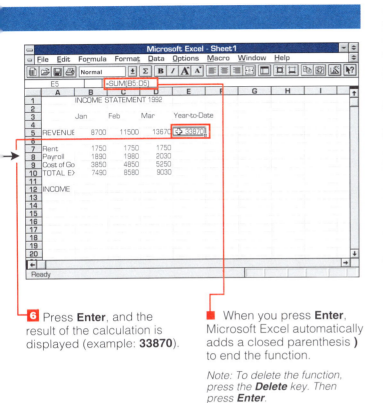

6 Press **Enter**, and the result of the calculation is displayed (example: **33870**).

■ When you press **Enter**, Microsoft Excel automatically adds a closed parenthesis **)** to end the function.

Note: To delete the function, press the **Delete** key. Then press **Enter**.

■ If **Circular:** appears at the bottom of the screen, the formula or function is included within its own range.

■ Always remove the circular reference before continuing.

■ Microsoft Excel tells you which cell contains the circular reference (example: **E10**).

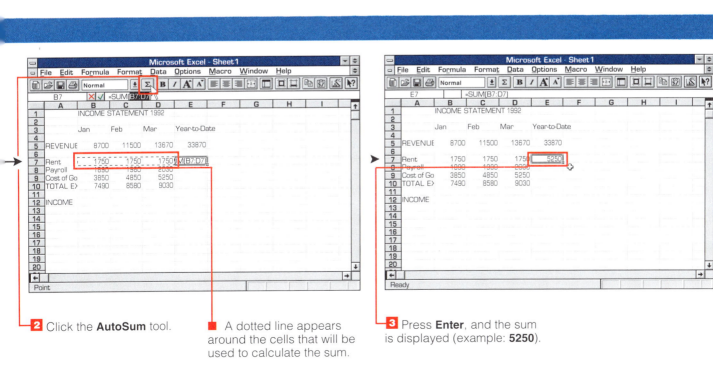

2 Click the **AutoSum** tool.

■ A dotted line appears around the cells that will be used to calculate the sum.

3 Press **Enter**, and the sum is displayed (example: **5250**).

29

AUTOFILL FUNCTIONS ABSOLUTE REFERENCES

AutoFill Functions

By using the AutoFill feature, Microsoft Excel can automatically copy a function to all selected cells.

1 Click the cell (example: E7) that contains the function you want to copy to other cells.

2 Move the mouse pointer ⊕ over the bottom right corner of the cell you want to copy and it changes to ✚.

3 Click and hold down the left mouse button as you drag the pointer ✚ over the cells you want to copy the function to.

Absolute References

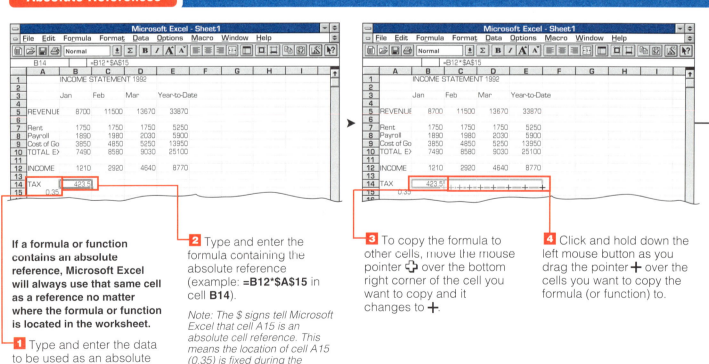

If a formula or function contains an absolute reference, Microsoft Excel will always use that same cell as a reference no matter where the formula or function is located in the worksheet.

1 Type and enter the data to be used as an absolute cell reference (example: **0.35** in cell **A15**).

2 Type and enter the formula containing the absolute reference (example: **=B12*A15** in cell **B14**).

Note: The $ signs tell Microsoft Excel that cell A15 is an absolute cell reference. This means the location of cell A15 (0.35) is fixed during the copying process.

3 To copy the formula to other cells, move the mouse pointer ⊕ over the bottom right corner of the cell you want to copy and it changes to ✚.

4 Click and hold down the left mouse button as you drag the pointer ✚ over the cells you want to copy the formula (or function) to.

30

| INTRODUCTION TO FORMULAS | ENTER FORMULAS | AUTOFILL FORMULAS | INTRODUCTION TO FUNCTIONS | ENTER FUNCTIONS | SUM USING THE AUTOSUM TOOL | **AUTOFILL FUNCTIONS** | **ABSOLUTE REFERENCES** |

4 Release the mouse button and the function is copied to all selected cells.

5 Select a cell (example: E9) that received a copy of the function.

■ Notice how the function was adjusted and the result recalculated for this cell.

6 To determine **Income**, click cell **B12** to select it. Type the formula **=B5-B10** (Revenue–Total Expenses), then press **Enter**. Use the AutoFill feature to copy the formula to cells **C12**, **D12** and **E12**.

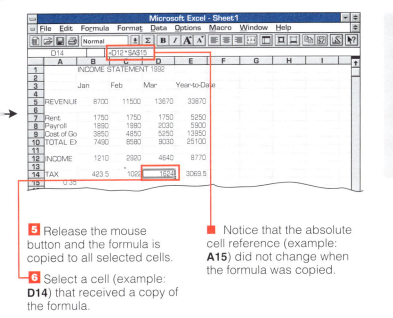

5 Release the mouse button and the formula is copied to all selected cells.

6 Select a cell (example: D14) that received a copy of the formula.

■ Notice that the absolute cell reference (example: A15) did not change when the formula was copied.

COPYING CELLS WITH ABSOLUTE REFERENCES

Example: **=B12*A15**

The first **$** sign tells Microsoft Excel that the column in the cell reference (example: **A**) is fixed. The second **$** sign tells Microsoft Excel that the row in the cell reference (example: **15**) is also fixed during the copy process.

GETTING STARTED

ENTER DATA

ENTER FORMULAS AND FUNCTIONS

MANAGING YOUR FILES

EDIT A WORKSHEET

FORMAT A WORKSHEET

CREATE AND EDIT A CHART

PRINT

OUTLINE A WORKSHEET

CREATE AND USE A DATABASE

31

FILES AND DIRECTORIES

HOW FILES ARE SPECIFIED

In an efficient and productive office environment, people create, edit, review and organize paper documents (example: letters, worksheets, reports, etc.). These documents are stored in folders, which in turn are placed in cabinets. To retrieve a specific document, you must identify it by location (cabinet and folder) and then by name.

Computers work the same way. After creating a document in Microsoft Excel, it must be named and saved. During the save process, you must tell Microsoft Excel the drive (cabinet) and directory (folder) the file is to reside in.

Microsoft Excel uses a multilevel directory filing system to store and retrieve your programs and data files. The first level of this directory structure is called the root directory. From this directory other sudirectories may be created. A typical multilevel filing system is illustrated on the next page.

Note: The terms "directory" and "subdirectory" are used interchangeably. The "root directory" is the only directory that cannot be called a "subdirectory".

File Specification

A file is specified by describing its drive, path and name (filename and extension).

C: \EXCEL\EXAMPLES\ INCOME92 .XLS

DRIVE
Tells Microsoft Excel the drive the file is in.

PATH
Tells Microsoft Excel the path through the directory structure to get to the file location.

FILENAME
The filename can contain up to 8 characters.

EXTENSION
The extension can contain up to 3 characters. In some cases, it is omitted.

Note: The first backslash (\) specifies the path to the root directory. Subsequent backslashes (\) are used to separate directories and the filename.

The following characters are allowed:

- The letters A to Z, upper or lower case
- The digits 0 through 9
- The underscore (_) and hyphen (-) characters
- The filename cannot contain a **.** (period) or blank spaces

| FILES AND DIRECTORIES | SAVE A WORKSHEET | CLOSE A WORKSHEET | OPEN A SAVED WORKSHEET | CREATE A NEW WORKSHEET | SWITCH BETWEEN WORKSHEETS | ARRANGE WORKSHEETS | DELETE A WORKSHEET |

Using Directories to Organize Your Files

■ Directories can contain files and/or paths to other directories. In this example, the root directory has paths to three subdirectories.

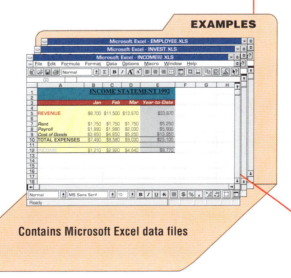

Contains Microsoft Excel data files

The file specification for this data file is:

C:\EXCEL\EXAMPLES\INCOME92.XLS

GETTING STARTED

ENTER DATA

ENTER FORMULAS AND FUNCTIONS

MANAGING YOUR FILES

EDIT A WORKSHEET

FORMAT A WORKSHEET

CREATE AND EDIT A CHART

PRINT

OUTLINE A WORKSHEET

CREATE AND USE A DATABASE

33

SAVE A WORKSHEET

Save a New Worksheet

A worksheet must be saved before exiting Microsoft Excel if it is required for future use.

1 Click **File** to open its menu.

Note: The Tax data was deleted from the worksheet. To delete data, refer to page 20.

2 Click **Save** and the **Save As** dialog box appears.

*Note: To save a previously saved worksheet with a new name, click **File**, then click **Save As**. Then follow steps* **3** *to* **5**

■ The worksheet will be saved to the current drive and directory (example: **c:\excel**).

3 In this example, the worksheet will be saved to the **examples** directory. To change to the **examples** directory, double click its name.

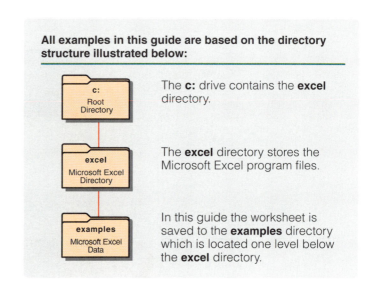

All examples in this guide are based on the directory structure illustrated below:

The **c:** drive contains the **excel** directory.

The **excel** directory stores the Microsoft Excel program files.

In this guide the worksheet is saved to the **examples** directory which is located one level below the **excel** directory.

| FILES AND DIRECTORIES | SAVE A WORKSHEET | CLOSE A WORKSHEET | OPEN A SAVED WORKSHEET | CREATE A NEW WORKSHEET | SWITCH BETWEEN WORKSHEETS | ARRANGE WORKSHEETS | DELETE A WORKSHEET |

4 Double click in the **File Name** box, then type a name for your worksheet (example: **INCOME92**).

5 Click the **OK** button.

Shortcut

To replace steps **3** to **5**, you can type the file specification (example: **c:\excel\examples\income92**) in the **File Name** box. Then press **Enter**.

■ The file (example: **INCOME92.XLS**) is saved.

*Note: If an extension is not specified, Microsoft Excel automatically adds the extension **.XLS**.*

 Save a Revised Worksheet

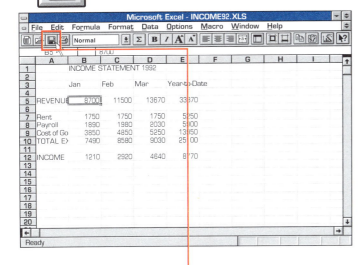

You should save regularly to prevent losing work due to power failure or hardware malfunctions.

1 Click the **Save File** tool to replace the previously saved version of the worksheet with the current one.

GETTING STARTED

ENTER DATA

ENTER FORMULAS AND FUNCTIONS

MANAGING YOUR FILES

EDIT A WORKSHEET

FORMAT A WORKSHEET

CREATE AND EDIT A CHART

PRINT

OUTLINE A WORKSHEET

CREATE AND USE A DATABASE

35

SAVE A WORKSHEET

CLOSE A WORKSHEET

Save a Worksheet to a Different Drive

1 Click **File** to open its menu.

2 Click **Save As** and the **Save As** dialog box appears.

Shortcut Press **F12**

■ The worksheet will be saved to the current drive and directory (example: **c:\excel\examples**).

3 To change the current drive, click the arrow beside the **Drives:** box and a list of all available drives is displayed.

4 Click the drive you want to save the worksheet to (example: **a:**).

Close a Worksheet

You can close a worksheet that is currently not in use.

1 Double click the **Control-menu** box of the worksheet you want to close.

■ The worksheet is closed.

■ Double clicking this **Control-menu** box exits Microsoft Excel and returns you to the Windows desktop.

| FILES AND DIRECTORIES | SAVE A WORKSHEET | CLOSE A WORKSHEET | OPEN A SAVED WORKSHEET | CREATE A NEW WORKSHEET | SWITCH BETWEEN WORKSHEETS | ARRANGE WORKSHEETS | DELETE A WORKSHEET |

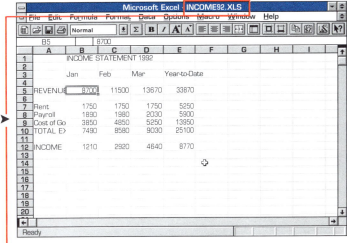

5 Double click in the **File Name** box, then type a name for your worksheet (example: **INCOME92**).

6 Click the **OK** button.

Shortcut

To replace steps **3** to **6**, you can type the file specification (example: **a:income92**) in the **File Name** box. Then press **Enter**.

■ The file (example: **INCOME92.XLS**) is saved to a different drive (example: **a:**).

*Note: If an extension is not specified, Microsoft Excel automatically adds the extension **.XLS**.*

GETTING STARTED

ENTER DATA

ENTER FORMULAS AND FUNCTIONS

MANAGING YOUR FILES

EDIT A WORKSHEET

FORMAT A WORKSHEET

CREATE AND EDIT A CHART

PRINT

OUTLINE A WORKSHEET

CREATE AND USE A DATABASE

If this dialog box appears when trying to close a worksheet, you have not saved changes you made to the worksheet.

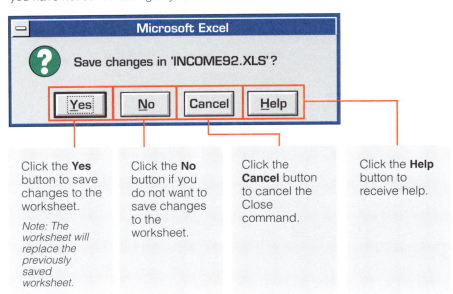

Click the **Yes** button to save changes to the worksheet.

Note: The worksheet will replace the previously saved worksheet.

Click the **No** button if you do not want to save changes to the worksheet.

Click the **Cancel** button to cancel the Close command.

Click the **Help** button to receive help.

37

OPEN A SAVED WORKSHEET   CREATE A NEW WORKSHEET   SWITCH BETWEEN WORKSHEETS

Open a Saved Worksheet

1 Click the **Open File** tool and the **Open** dialog box appears.

■ The current drive and directory are displayed (example: **a:**).

Note: The current drive and directory are the same as the last drive and directory that were opened or saved to.

2 To change the current drive, click the arrow beside the **Drives:** box and a list of all available drives is displayed.

3 Click the drive you want to change to (example: **c:**).

■ The files in the current drive and directory are displayed.

Note: To change the current directory, double click the directory you want to make current.

4 Click the name of the file you want to open (example: **income92.xls**).

5 Click the **OK** button, or press **Enter**.

Create a New Worksheet

1 Click the **New Worksheet** tool.

■ A new worksheet appears.

*Note: The **INCOME92.XLS** worksheet is hidden behind the new worksheet.*

| FILES AND DIRECTORIES | SAVE A WORKSHEET | CLOSE A WORKSHEET | **OPEN A SAVED WORKSHEET** | **CREATE A NEW WORKSHEET** | **SWITCH BETWEEN WORKSHEETS** | ARRANGE WORKSHEETS | DELETE A WORKSHEET |

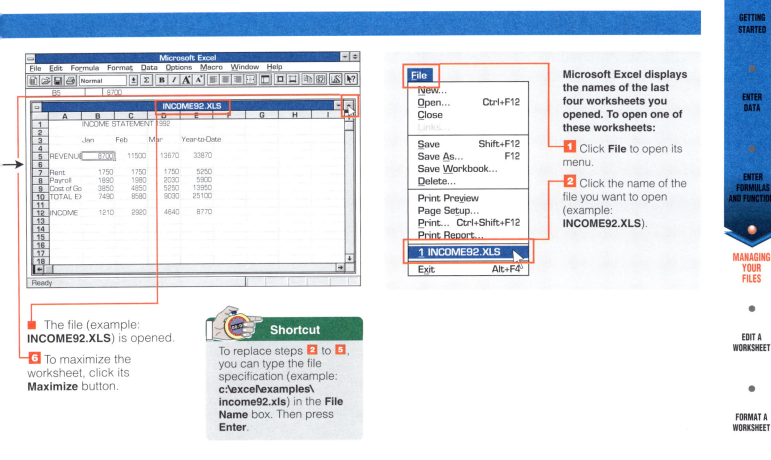

- The file (example: **INCOME92.XLS**) is opened.
- **6** To maximize the worksheet, click its **Maximize** button.

Shortcut
To replace steps **2** to **5**, you can type the file specification (example: **c:\excel\examples\income92.xls**) in the **File Name** box. Then press **Enter**.

Microsoft Excel displays the names of the last four worksheets you opened. To open one of these worksheets:

1 Click **File** to open its menu.

2 Click the name of the file you want to open (example: **INCOME92.XLS**).

Switch Between Worksheets

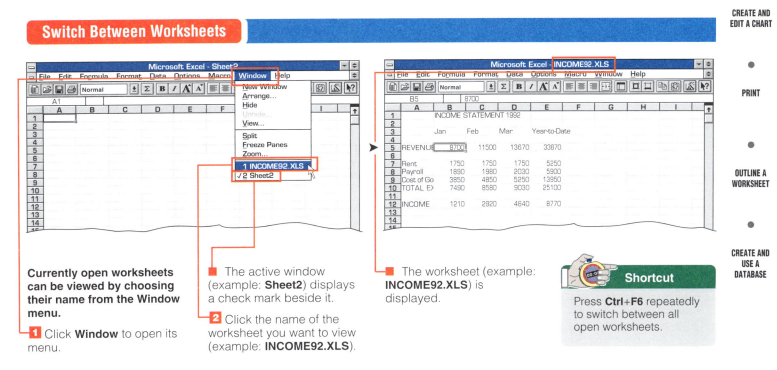

Currently open worksheets can be viewed by choosing their name from the Window menu.

1 Click **Window** to open its menu.

- The active window (example: **Sheet2**) displays a check mark beside it.

2 Click the name of the worksheet you want to view (example: **INCOME92.XLS**).

- The worksheet (example: **INCOME92.XLS**) is displayed.

Shortcut
Press **Ctrl+F6** repeatedly to switch between all open worksheets.

GETTING STARTED

ENTER DATA

ENTER FORMULAS AND FUNCTIONS

MANAGING YOUR FILES

EDIT A WORKSHEET

FORMAT A WORKSHEET

CREATE AND EDIT A CHART

PRINT

OUTLINE A WORKSHEET

CREATE AND USE A DATABASE

39

ARRANGE WORKSHEETS   DELETE A WORKSHEET

Arrange Worksheets

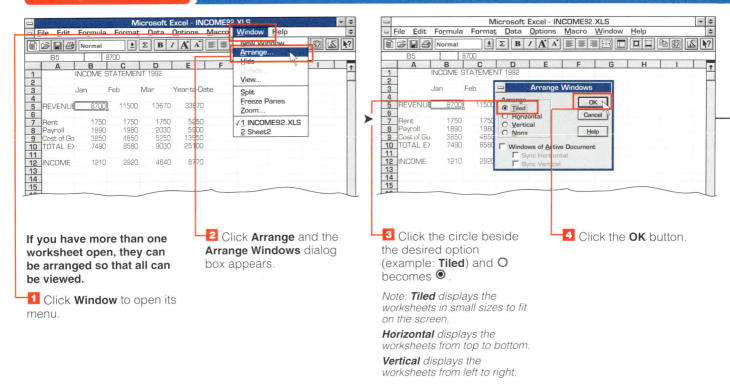

If you have more than one worksheet open, they can be arranged so that all can be viewed.

1 Click **Window** to open its menu.

2 Click **Arrange** and the **Arrange Windows** dialog box appears.

3 Click the circle beside the desired option (example: **Tiled**) and O becomes ⊙.

Note: **Tiled** displays the worksheets in small sizes to fit on the screen.

Horizontal displays the worksheets from top to bottom.

Vertical displays the worksheets from left to right.

4 Click the **OK** button.

Delete a Worksheet

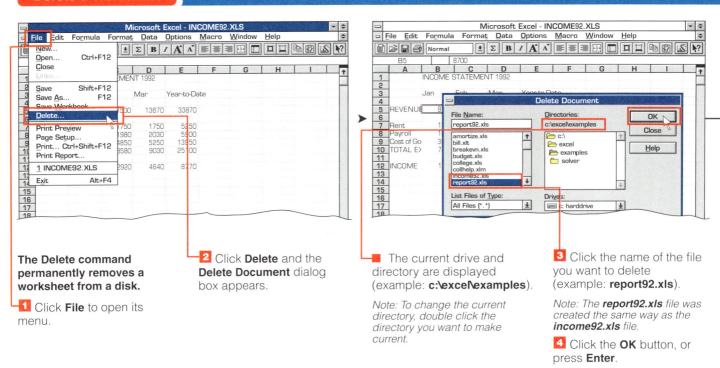

The Delete command permanently removes a worksheet from a disk.

1 Click **File** to open its menu.

2 Click **Delete** and the **Delete Document** dialog box appears.

■ The current drive and directory are displayed (example: **c:\excel\examples**).

Note: To change the current directory, double click the directory you want to make current.

3 Click the name of the file you want to delete (example: **report92.xls**).

Note: The **report92.xls** file was created the same way as the **income92.xls** file.

4 Click the **OK** button, or press **Enter**.

40

| FILES AND DIRECTORIES | SAVE A WORKSHEET | CLOSE A WORKSHEET | OPEN A SAVED WORKSHEET | CREATE A NEW WORKSHEET | SWITCH BETWEEN WORKSHEETS | **ARRANGE WORKSHEETS** | **DELETE A WORKSHEET** |

GETTING STARTED

ENTER DATA

ENTER FORMULAS AND FUNCTIONS

MANAGING YOUR FILES

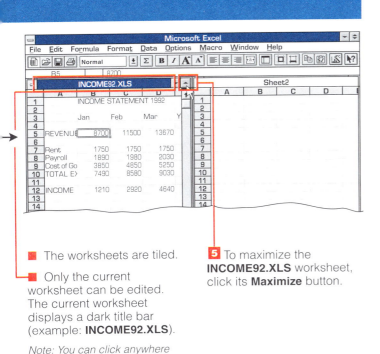

■ The worksheets are tiled.

■ Only the current worksheet can be edited. The current worksheet displays a dark title bar (example: **INCOME92.XLS**).

Note: You can click anywhere on any worksheet to make it current.

5 To maximize the **INCOME92.XLS** worksheet, click its **Maximize** button.

EDIT A WORKSHEET

FORMAT A WORKSHEET

■ This dialog box appears offering you one last chance to change your mind.

5 To delete the file, click the **Yes** button.

*Note: If you do not want to delete the file, click the **No** button.*

■ The file (example: **report92.xls**) is deleted.

6 To close the **Delete Document** dialog box, click the **Close** button.

Shortcut

To replace steps **3** to **5**, you can type the file specification (example: **c:\excel\examples\report92.xls**) in the **File Name** box. Then press **Enter**.

CREATE AND EDIT A CHART

PRINT

OUTLINE A WORKSHEET

CREATE AND USE A DATABASE

41

CHANGE COLUMN WIDTH

Change the Width of One Column

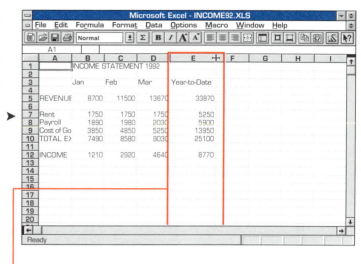

1 To change the width of a column (example: **E**), move the mouse pointer ✥ over the right edge of the column heading and it changes to ✚.

2 Click and hold down the left mouse button as you drag the border to the desired width.

3 Release the mouse button and the column width is changed.

Note: When a number is too long to fit in a cell, Microsoft Excel tries to display it exponentially.

If the exponential form is still too long, number signs (###) are displayed in the cell.

To display the whole number, increase the column width.

Change the Width of Many Columns

By changing the width of several columns at the same time, each selected column will end up displaying the same column width.

1 Click the column heading of the first column you want to change (example: **B**).

2 To select multiple adjacent columns, hold down the **Shift** key, then click the column heading of the last column you want to change (example: **D**). Release the **Shift** key.

*Note: To select nonadjacent columns, hold down the **Ctrl** key, then click the column headings you want to select.*

| CHANGE COLUMN WIDTH | CHANGE ROW HEIGHT | INSERT OR DELETE A ROW | INSERT OR DELETE A COLUMN | MOVE OR COPY DATA |

Best Fit the Width of One Column

With Microsoft Excel you can easily change the column width to best fit the longest item in the column.

1 To best fit the width of a column (example: **A**), move the mouse pointer ✥ over the right edge of the column heading and it changes to ✥.

2 Double click the left mouse button.

■ The column width is changed to best fit the longest cell entry in the column (example: **TOTAL EXPENSES**).

3 To change the column width of all selected columns, move the mouse pointer ✥ over the right edge of any selected column heading (example: **D**) and it changes to ✥.

4 Click and hold down the left mouse button as you drag the border to the desired width.

5 Release the mouse button and all selected columns display the same column width.

- GETTING STARTED
- ENTER DATA
- ENTER FORMULAS AND FUNCTIONS
- MANAGING YOUR FILES
- EDIT A WORKSHEET
- FORMAT A WORKSHEET
- CREATE AND EDIT A CHART
- PRINT
- OUTLINE A WORKSHEET
- CREATE AND USE A DATABASE

43

CHANGE ROW HEIGHT

Change the Height of One Row

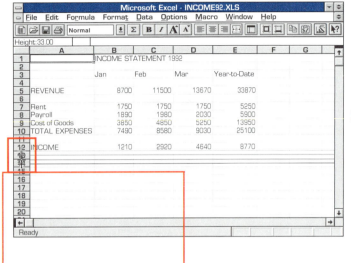

1 To change the height of a row (example: **12**), move the mouse pointer ✥ to the bottom edge of the row heading and it changes to ✢.

2 Click and hold down the left mouse button as you drag the border to the desired height.

3 Release the mouse button and the row height is changed.

Change the Height of Many Rows

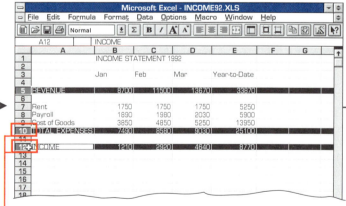

By changing the height of several rows at the same time, each selected row will end up displaying the same row height.

1 Click the row heading of the first row you want to change (example: **5**).

2 To select multiple nonadjacent rows, hold down the **Ctrl** key, then click the row headings you want to select (example: **10** and **12**). Release the **Ctrl** key.

Note: To select adjacent rows, hold down the **Shift** key, then click the row heading of the last row you want to select. Release the **Shift** key.

| CHANGE COLUMN WIDTH | **CHANGE ROW HEIGHT** | INSERT OR DELETE A ROW | INSERT OR DELETE A COLUMN | MOVE OR COPY DATA |

Best Fit the Height of One Row

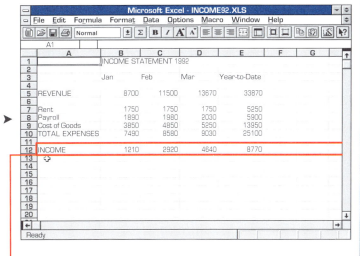

With Microsoft Excel you can easily change the row height to best fit the tallest item in the row.

1 To best fit the height of a row (example: **12**), move the mouse pointer ✣ to the bottom edge of the row heading and it changes to ✢.

2 Double click the left mouse button.

■ The row height is changed to best fit the tallest cell entry in the row.

3 To change the row height of all selected rows, move the mouse pointer ✣ over the bottom edge of any selected row heading (example: **5**) and it changes to ✢.

4 Click and hold down the left mouse button as you drag the border to the desired height.

5 Release the mouse button and all selected rows display the same row height.

GETTING STARTED

ENTER DATA

ENTER FORMULAS AND FUNCTIONS

MANAGING YOUR FILES

EDIT A WORKSHEET

FORMAT A WORKSHEET

CREATE AND EDIT A CHART

PRINT

OUTLINE A WORKSHEET

CREATE AND USE A DATABASE

45

INSERT OR DELETE A ROW

INSERT OR DELETE A COLUMN

Insert a Row

Microsoft Excel inserts a new row above the selected row.

1 Select the row you want to move downward to make room for a new row. To select a row (example: **4**), click its row heading.

2 Move the mouse pointer ✥ anywhere over the selected row. Then click the **right** mouse button. A shortcut menu appears.

3 Click **Insert**.

■ A new row is inserted.

Delete a Row

1 Click the row heading of the row you want to delete (example: **4**).

2 Move the mouse pointer ✥ anywhere over the selected row. Then click the **right** mouse button. A shortcut menu appears.

3 Click **Delete**.

■ The row is deleted.

Note: If **#REF!** appears in a cell on your worksheet, this indicates that you deleted a row that contained information needed to calculate a formula or function.

Note: To cancel the deletion, click **Edit**. Then click **Undo Delete**. This only works immediately after a row is deleted.

CHANGE COLUMN WIDTH | CHANGE ROW HEIGHT | **INSERT OR DELETE A ROW** | **INSERT OR DELETE A COLUMN** | MOVE OR COPY DATA

Insert a Column

Microsoft Excel inserts a new column to the left of the selected column.

1 Select the column you want to move to the right to make room for a new column. To select a column (example: **E**), click its column heading.

2 Move the mouse pointer ✥ anywhere over the selected column. Then click the **right** mouse button. A shortcut menu appears.

3 Click **Insert**.

■ A new column is inserted.

Delete a Column

 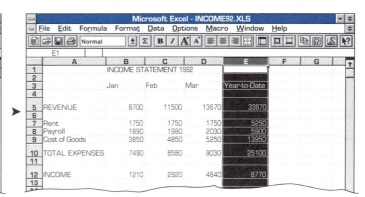

1 Click the column heading of the column you want to delete (example: **E**).

2 Move the mouse pointer ✥ anywhere over the selected column. Then click the **right** mouse button. A shortcut menu appears.

3 Click **Delete**.

■ The column is deleted.

Note: If **#REF!** appears in a cell on your worksheet, this indicates that you deleted a column that contained information needed to calculate a formula or function.

Note: To cancel the deletion, click **Edit**. Then click **Undo Delete**. This only works immediately after a column is deleted.

GETTING STARTED

ENTER DATA

ENTER FORMULAS AND FUNCTIONS

MANAGING YOUR FILES

EDIT A WORKSHEET

FORMAT A WORKSHEET

CREATE AND EDIT A CHART

PRINT

OUTLINE A WORKSHEET

CREATE AND USE A DATABASE

47

MOVE OR COPY DATA

Move Data

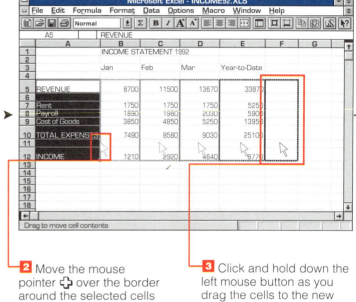

1 Select the cells you want to move to a new location.

Note: To select cells, refer to page 10.

2 Move the mouse pointer ✛ over the border around the selected cells and it changes to ↖.

3 Click and hold down the left mouse button as you drag the cells to the new location.

Copy Data

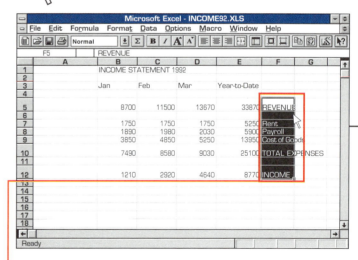

1 Select the cells you want to copy to a new location.

Note: To select cells, refer to page 10.

48

CHANGE COLUMN WIDTH   CHANGE ROW HEIGHT   INSERT OR DELETE A ROW   INSERT OR DELETE A COLUMN   **MOVE OR COPY DATA**

- GETTING STARTED
- ENTER DATA
- ENTER FORMULAS AND FUNCTIONS
- MANAGING YOUR FILES
- **EDIT A WORKSHEET**
- FORMAT A WORKSHEET
- CREATE AND EDIT A CHART
- PRINT
- OUTLINE A WORKSHEET
- CREATE AND USE A DATABASE

4 Release the mouse button and the data is moved.

2 Move the mouse pointer over the border around the selected cells and it changes to ⇖.

3 Press and hold down the **Ctrl** key and ⇖ changes to ⇖.

4 Still holding down the **Ctrl** key, click and hold down the left mouse button as you drag the cells to the new location.

5 Release the mouse button, then the **Ctrl** key, and the data is copied.

49

MOVE OR COPY DATA

Move or Copy Data to Another Worksheet

1 Select the cells you want to move (or copy) to a new location.

Note: To select cells, refer to page 10.

2 Move the mouse pointer ✣ anywhere over the selected cells. Then click the **right** mouse button. A shortcut menu appears.

3 To move the selected cells, click **Cut**.

or

To copy the selected cells, click **Copy**.

4 To move (or copy) the data to a new worksheet, click the **New Worksheet** tool to open a new worksheet.

Note: You can also move (or copy) data to a saved worksheet by opening that worksheet. To open a saved worksheet, refer to page 38.

Rather than choosing a command from the main menu bar, you can use the **right** mouse button to display a shortcut menu.

A shortcut menu displays the most useful commands for that cell, cell range or object.

To display a shortcut menu, click the **right** mouse button over a selection or object.

| CHANGE COLUMN WIDTH | CHANGE ROW HEIGHT | INSERT OR DELETE A ROW | INSERT OR DELETE A COLUMN | **MOVE OR COPY DATA** |

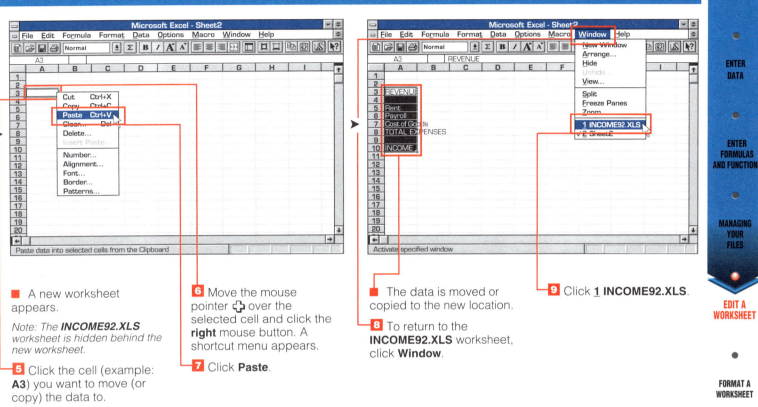

- A new worksheet appears.

  Note: The **INCOME92.XLS** worksheet is hidden behind the new worksheet.

  5 Click the cell (example: **A3**) you want to move (or copy) the data to.

  Note: The selected cell is used as the top left corner cell of the new location.

6 Move the mouse pointer ✥ over the selected cell and click the **right** mouse button. A shortcut menu appears.

7 Click **Paste**.

- The data is moved or copied to the new location.

8 To return to the **INCOME92.XLS** worksheet, click **Window**.

9 Click **1 INCOME92.XLS**.

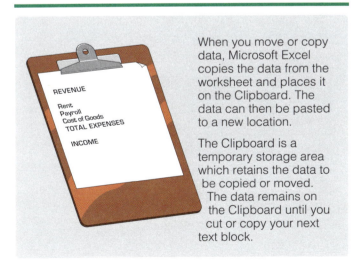

When you move or copy data, Microsoft Excel copies the data from the worksheet and places it on the Clipboard. The data can then be pasted to a new location.

The Clipboard is a temporary storage area which retains the data to be copied or moved. The data remains on the Clipboard until you cut or copy your next text block.

GETTING STARTED

ENTER DATA

ENTER FORMULAS AND FUNCTIONS

MANAGING YOUR FILES

EDIT A WORKSHEET

FORMAT A WORKSHEET

CREATE AND EDIT A CHART

PRINT

OUTLINE A WORKSHEET

CREATE AND USE A DATABASE

51

DISPLAY OR HIDE A TOOLBAR

FORMAT NUMBERS

Display or Hide a Toolbar

Toolbars contain tools that help you perform tasks quickly and more easily. Microsoft Excel offers the following toolbars:

TOOLBAR	DESCRIPTION
Standard	Contains tools for some of the most frequently used commands.
Formatting	Changes shape, size and general appearance of data.
Utility	Contains miscellaneous tools.
Chart	Changes chart appearance.
Drawing	Draws shapes, lines, and adds color.
Microsoft Excel 3.0	Contains the same tools as the Microsoft Excel Version 3.0 toolbar.

Note: The **Macro** toolbar is for advanced users. For more information, refer to your Microsoft Excel User's Guides.

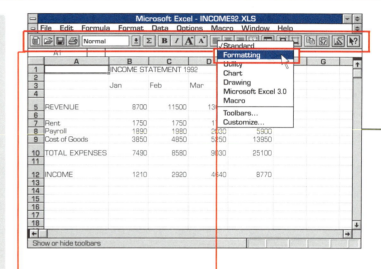

1 Move the mouse pointer ✛ anywhere over the **Standard** toolbar and it changes to ↖.

Note: The **Standard** toolbar automatically appears when you first start Microsoft Excel.

2 Click the **right** mouse button and a shortcut menu appears.

3 Click the name of the toolbar (example: **Formatting**) you want to display.

Note: A checkmark (✓) beside a toolbar name indicates it is already displayed. Click this toolbar name if you wish to hide it.

Format Numbers

1 Select the cells that contain the numbers you want to format.

Note: To select cells, refer to page 10.

2 Click the arrow beside the **Style Box** and a list of the available styles appears.

Note: You can use the **Style Box** on the **Standard** toolbar, or on the **Formatting** toolbar.

3 Click the desired number style (example: **Currency [0]**).

Style Options	Shown As
Comma	1,000.00
Comma [0]	1,000
Currency	$1,000.00
Currency [0]	$1,000
Normal	1000
Percent	100000%

52

| DISPLAY OR HIDE A TOOLBAR | FORMAT NUMBERS | CHANGE FONTS | ALIGN DATA | BORDERS AND SHADING | REMOVE FORMATS | COPY AND PASTE FORMATS | BOLD, ITALIC, AND UNDERLINE | AUTOFORMAT | THE DRAWING TOOLBAR |

- The toolbar (example: **Formatting**) is displayed.

4 To reposition the toolbar, move the mouse pointer over a blank area in the toolbar. Click the left mouse button and hold it down.

5 Still holding down the button, drag the toolbar to where you want it positioned.

6 Release the mouse button and the toolbar jumps to its new position.

Note: If you drag a toolbar to the top or bottom edge of the screen, it lines up along that edge.

*Note: If you accidentally hide all the toolbars, click **Options**, then click **Toolbars**. Double click the name of the toolbar you want to display.*

- The numbers are displayed in the new format.

Note: If number signs (###) appear in a cell, the column width is not wide enough to display the new number format. To change the column width, refer to page 42.

FORMAT NUMBERS USING THE FORMATTING TOOLS

1 Select the cells that contain the numbers you want to format.

2 Click the desired format tool:

- $ Currency (2 decimal places)
- % Percent (0 decimal places)
- , Comma (2 decimal places)
- Add 1 decimal place to a number
- Remove 1 decimal place from a number

GETTING STARTED

ENTER DATA

ENTER FORMULAS AND FUNCTIONS

MANAGING YOUR FILES

EDIT A WORKSHEET

FORMAT A WORKSHEET

CREATE AND EDIT A CHART

PRINT

OUTLINE A WORKSHEET

CREATE AND USE A DATABASE

53

CHANGE FONTS

Change Fonts

A font defines the design of displayed characters.

1 Select the cell(s) that contains the data you want to change to a new font (example: **B1**).

Note: To select cells, refer to page 10.

2 Click the arrow beside the **Font Name Box** and a list of the available fonts appears.

*Note: The **Font Name Box** is on the **Formatting** toolbar.*

3 To view more fonts, click the up or down scroll arrow.

4 Click the desired font name (example: **Times New Roman**).

Increase or Decrease Font Size

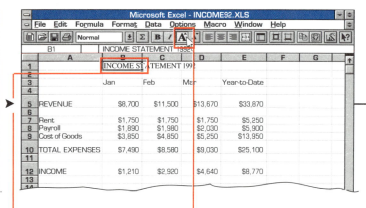

1 Select the cell(s) that contains the data you want to change to a new font size.

2 To increase the font size, click the **Increase Font Size** tool.

*Note: To decrease the font size, click the **Decrease Font Size** tool.*

■ The size of the text is changed.

Note: The size of numbers can also be changed.

3 Continue clicking a **Font Size** tool until the desired size is reached (example: click the **Increase Font Size** tool twice to move up two font sizes).

54

| DISPLAY OR HIDE A TOOLBAR | FORMAT NUMBERS | **CHANGE FONTS** | ALIGN DATA | BORDERS AND SHADING | REMOVE FORMATS | COPY AND PASTE FORMATS | BOLD, ITALIC, AND UNDERLINE | AUTOFORMAT | THE DRAWING TOOLBAR |

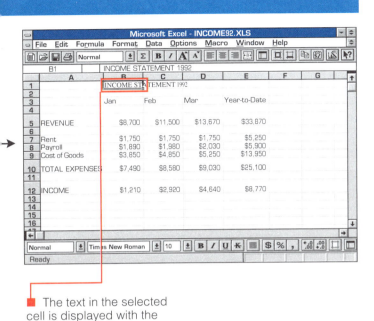

■ The text in the selected cell is displayed with the new font.

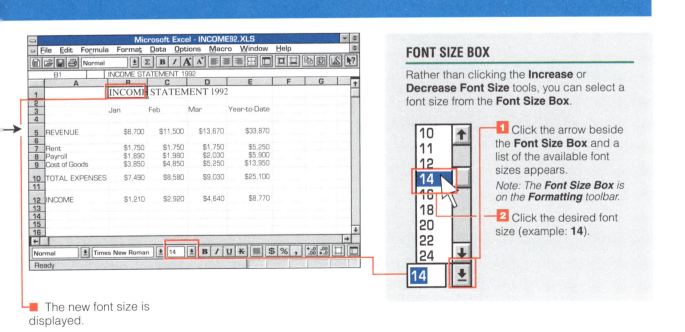

■ The new font size is displayed.

FONT SIZE BOX

Rather than clicking the **Increase** or **Decrease Font Size** tools, you can select a font size from the **Font Size Box**.

1 Click the arrow beside the **Font Size Box** and a list of the available font sizes appears.

Note: The **Font Size Box** is on the **Formatting** toolbar.

2 Click the desired font size (example: **14**).

ALIGN DATA

Left   Center   Right Align

With Microsoft Excel you can left align, right align, or center data in each cell.

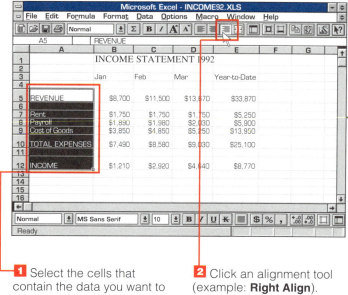

1 Select the cells that contain the data you want to align.

Note: To select cells, refer to page 10.

2 Click an alignment tool (example: **Right Align**).

*Note: The alignment tools are on the **Standard** toolbar.*

Center Text Across Selected Columns

1 Select the cells you want the text to be centered between.

Note: Make sure the text you want to center across columns is in the far left selected cell.

2 Click the **Center Across Columns** tool.

*Note: This tool is on the **Standard** toolbar.*

| DISPLAY OR HIDE A TOOLBAR | FORMAT NUMBERS | CHANGE FONTS | **ALIGN DATA** | BORDERS AND SHADING | REMOVE FORMATS | COPY AND PASTE FORMATS | BOLD, ITALIC, AND UNDERLINE | AUTOFORMAT | THE DRAWING TOOLBAR |

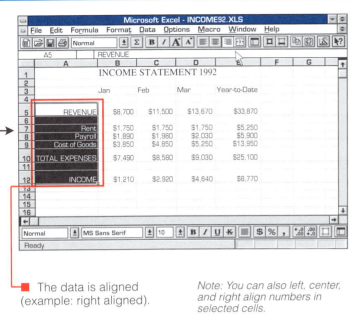

■ The data is aligned (example: right aligned).

Note: You can also left, center, and right align numbers in selected cells.

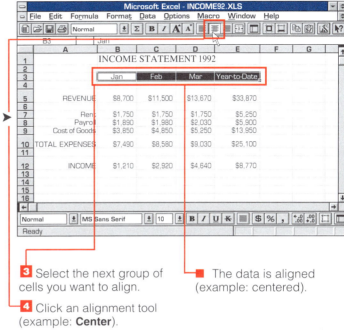

3 Select the next group of cells you want to align.

4 Click an alignment tool (example: **Center**).

■ The data is aligned (example: centered).

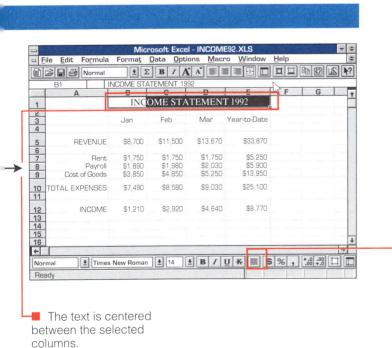

■ The text is centered between the selected columns.

JUSTIFY ALIGN TOOL

Rather than having long text spill into adjacent cells, text can be justified to fit into one cell.

1 Select the cell that contains the text you want to justify.

2 Click the **Justify Align** tool.

Note: This tool is on the Formatting toolbar.

57

BORDERS AND SHADING   REMOVE FORMATS

Add Borders

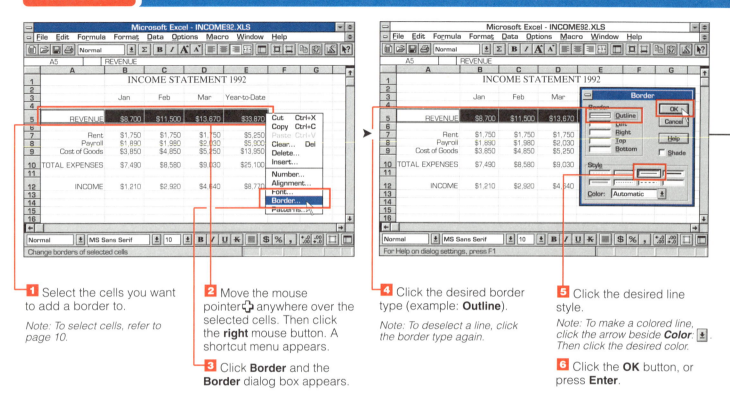

1 Select the cells you want to add a border to.

Note: To select cells, refer to page 10.

2 Move the mouse pointer ✥ anywhere over the selected cells. Then click the **right** mouse button. A shortcut menu appears.

3 Click **Border** and the **Border** dialog box appears.

4 Click the desired border type (example: **Outline**).

Note: To deselect a line, click the border type again.

5 Click the desired line style.

*Note: To make a colored line, click the arrow beside **Color**. Then click the desired color.*

6 Click the **OK** button, or press **Enter**.

Add Shading

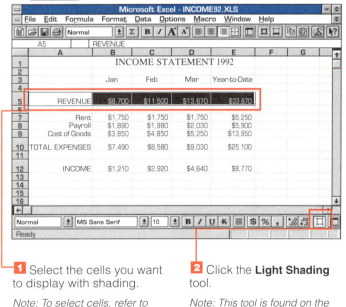

1 Select the cells you want to display with shading.

Note: To select cells, refer to page 10.

2 Click the **Light Shading** tool.

*Note: This tool is found on the **Formatting** toolbar.*

3 Click a cell outside the selected cell range (example: **A14**) so you can clearly view the shading.

■ The cells display the light shading pattern.

| DISPLAY OR HIDE A TOOLBAR | FORMAT NUMBERS | CHANGE FONTS | ALIGN DATA | **BORDERS AND SHADING** | **REMOVE FORMATS** | COPY AND PASTE FORMATS | BOLD, ITALIC, AND UNDERLINE | AUTOFORMAT | THE DRAWING TOOLBAR |

 OUTLINE BORDER TOOL

To quickly add a border along the outermost edges of selected cells:

1 Select the cells you want to add the border to.

2 Click the **Outline Border** tool.

Note: This tool is found on the Standard toolbar.

 BOTTOM BORDER TOOL

To quickly add a border along the bottom edge of selected cells:

1 Select the cells you want to add the border to.

2 Click the **Bottom Border** tool.

Note: This tool is found on the Standard toolbar.

7 Click a cell outside the selected cell range (example: **A14**) so you can clearly view the border.

■ The border is displayed.

 Remove Formats

1 Select the cells that contain the formatting you want to remove.

Note: To select cells, refer to page 10.

2 Press the **Delete** key and the **Clear** dialog box appears.

3 Click the circle beside **Formats** and ○ becomes ◉.

4 Click the **OK** button, or press **Enter**.

5 Click a cell outside the selected cell range (example: **A14**) so you can clearly see that all formatting was removed.

■ All formats are cleared from the selected cells. The data within the cells does not change.

6 To quickly undo the remove formats command, press **Ctrl+Z**.

Note: You can also undo the remove formats command by using the Main menu. Click Edit, then click Undo Clear.

COPY AND PASTE FORMATS

BOLD, ITALIC, AND UNDERLINE

Copy and Paste Formats

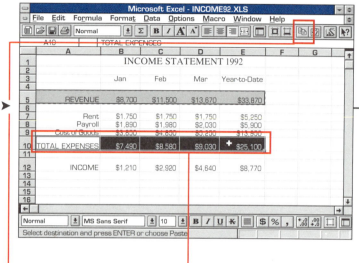

You can apply current formats quickly and consistently to selected cells by using the **Copy and Paste Formats** tools.

1 Select the cells that contain the format attributes you want to copy to other cells.

2 Click the **Copy Formats** tool.

Note: A moving border appears around the cells to be copied.

3 Select the cells you want to apply the format to.

Bold

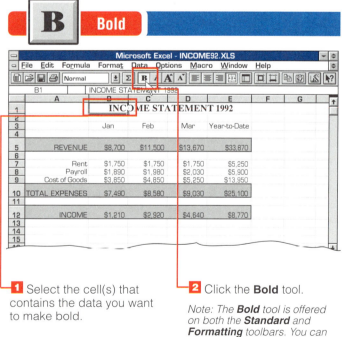

1 Select the cell(s) that contains the data you want to make bold.

2 Click the **Bold** tool.

*Note: The **Bold** tool is offered on both the **Standard** and **Formatting** toolbars. You can click either tool.*

*To remove the bold formatting from selected cells, click the **Bold** tool again.*

Italic

1 Select the cells that contain the data you want to make italic.

2 Click the **Italic** tool.

*Note: The **Italic** tool is offered on both the **Standard** and **Formatting** toolbars. You can click either tool.*

*To remove the italic formatting from selected cells, click the **Italic** tool again.*

60

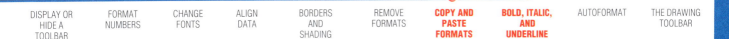

| DISPLAY OR HIDE A TOOLBAR | FORMAT NUMBERS | CHANGE FONTS | ALIGN DATA | BORDERS AND SHADING | REMOVE FORMATS | **COPY AND PASTE FORMATS** | **BOLD, ITALIC, AND UNDERLINE** | AUTOFORMAT | THE DRAWING TOOLBAR |

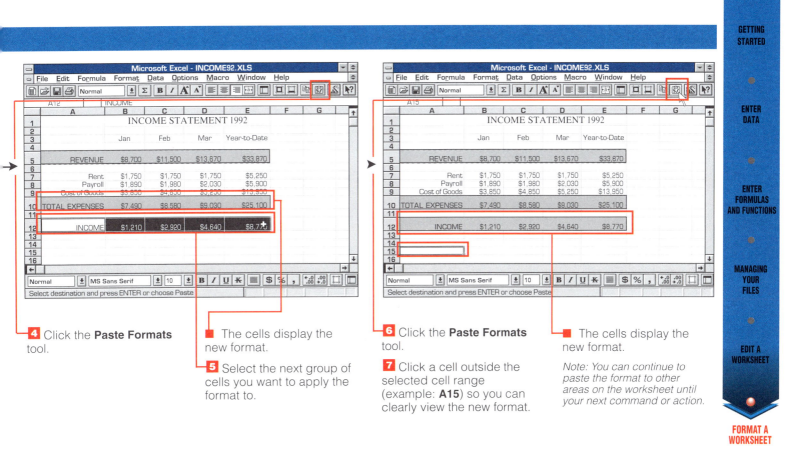

4 Click the **Paste Formats** tool.

■ The cells display the new format.

5 Select the next group of cells you want to apply the format to.

6 Click the **Paste Formats** tool.

7 Click a cell outside the selected cell range (example: **A15**) so you can clearly view the new format.

■ The cells display the new format.

Note: You can continue to paste the format to other areas on the worksheet until your next command or action.

Underline

1 Select the cell(s) that contains the data you want to underline.

2 Click the **Underline** tool on the **Formatting** toolbar.

*Note: To remove the underline formatting from selected cells, click the **Underline** tool again.*

STRIKEOUT TOOL

Example: ~~This is strikeout text~~.

1 Select the cells that contain the data you want to place a line through.

2 Click the **Strikeout** tool on the **Formatting** toolbar.

*Note: To remove the strikeout formatting from selected cells, click the **Strikeout** tool again.*

61

AUTOFORMAT

AutoFormat

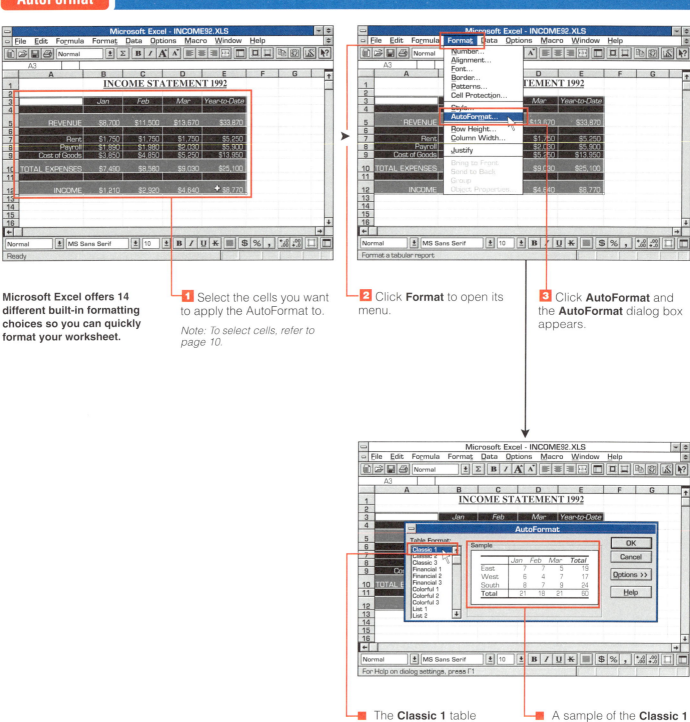

Microsoft Excel offers 14 different built-in formatting choices so you can quickly format your worksheet.

1 Select the cells you want to apply the AutoFormat to.

Note: To select cells, refer to page 10.

2 Click **Format** to open its menu.

3 Click **AutoFormat** and the **AutoFormat** dialog box appears.

■ The **Classic 1** table format is the current selection.

■ A sample of the **Classic 1** AutoFormat appears in the **Sample** box.

| DISPLAY OR HIDE A TOOLBAR | FORMAT NUMBERS | CHANGE FONTS | ALIGN DATA | BORDERS AND SHADING | REMOVE FORMATS | COPY AND PASTE FORMATS | BOLD, ITALIC, AND UNDERLINE | **AUTOFORMAT** | THE DRAWING TOOLBAR |

5 Click another **Table Format** (example: **Colorful 2**).

■ A sample of the selected AutoFormat appears in the **Sample** box.

6 Click the **OK** button, or press **Enter** to choose that AutoFormat.

7 Click a cell outside the selected cell range (example: **A15**) so you can clearly view the new format.

■ The worksheet data is formatted to display the format you chose.

*Note: For the remainder of this book the **Formatting** toolbar is hidden. To remove a toolbar from the screen, refer to page 52.*

4 Click another **Table Format** (example: **List 2**).

■ A sample of the selected AutoFormat appears in the **Sample** box.

AUTOFORMAT TOOL

If you make changes to your worksheet, you can quickly apply your last table format using the AutoFormat tool.

1 Select the cells you want to apply the AutoFormat to.

2 Click the **AutoFormat** tool.

*Note: This tool is on both the **Standard** and **Formatting** toolbars.*

63

THE DRAWING TOOLBAR

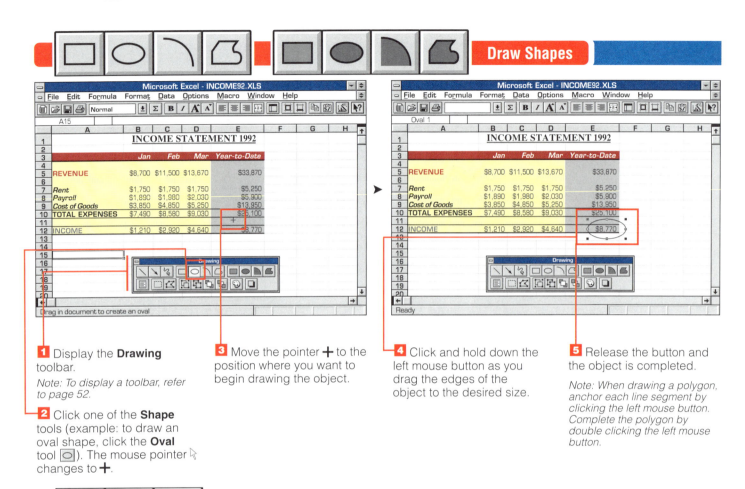

Draw Shapes

1 Display the **Drawing** toolbar.

Note: To display a toolbar, refer to page 52.

2 Click one of the **Shape** tools (example: to draw an oval shape, click the **Oval** tool). The mouse pointer changes to +.

3 Move the pointer + to the position where you want to begin drawing the object.

4 Click and hold down the left mouse button as you drag the edges of the object to the desired size.

5 Release the button and the object is completed.

Note: When drawing a polygon, anchor each line segment by clicking the left mouse button. Complete the polygon by double clicking the left mouse button.

Draw Lines

1 Click one of the **Line** tools (example: to draw an arrow, click the **Arrow** tool). The mouse pointer changes to +.

2 Move the pointer + to the position where you want to begin drawing the line.

3 Click and hold down the left mouse button as you drag the line to the desired length.

4 Release the button and the line is completed.

| DISPLAY OR HIDE A TOOLBAR | FORMAT NUMBERS | CHANGE FONTS | ALIGN DATA | BORDERS AND SHADING | REMOVE FORMATS | COPY AND PASTE FORMATS | BOLD, ITALIC, AND UNDERLINE | AUTOFORMAT | **THE DRAWING TOOLBAR** |

 Add Color

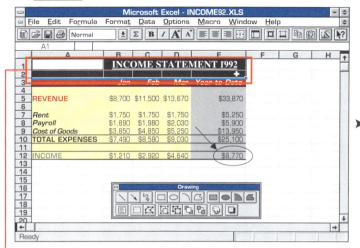

1 Select the cells or object you want to add color to.

Note: To select an object, move the mouse pointer ✛ over one of the object's edges and it changes to ↖. Click the left mouse button.

2 Click the **Color** tool several times until the desired color appears in the top left corner of the selected cells (example: click the **Color** tool 14 times to display the color shown in the above screen).

3 Click a cell outside the selected cell range (example: **G3**) so you can clearly view the new color.

*Note: If you passed by the color you wanted to choose, don't worry. Continue clicking the **Color** tool and the color will appear again.*

 Delete an Object

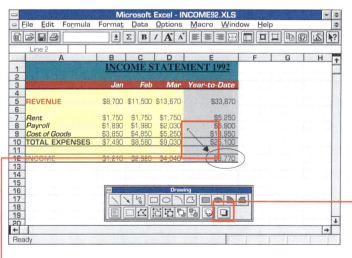

1 To select the object you want to delete, move the mouse pointer ✛ over one of the object's edges and it changes to ↖. Click the left mouse button.

2 Press the **Delete** key.

*Note: For the remainder of this book the **Drawing** toolbar is hidden. To remove a toolbar from the screen, refer to page 52.*

ADD OUTLINE AND DROP SHADOW USING THIS TOOL

1 Select the cells you want to add an outline and drop shadow to.

2 Click the **Drop Shadow** tool.

65

CREATE A CHART

The ChartWizard leads you through five steps to create a chart using data from your worksheet.

In this example, the Revenue and Total Expenses for the months of Jan, Feb, and Mar will be charted.

Data Range to be Charted (Step 1 of 5)

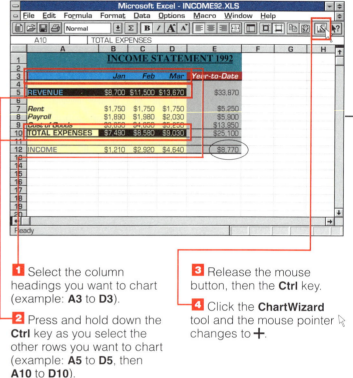

1 Select the column headings you want to chart (example: **A3** to **D3**).

2 Press and hold down the **Ctrl** key as you select the other rows you want to chart (example: **A5** to **D5**, then **A10** to **D10**).

3 Release the mouse button, then the **Ctrl** key.

4 Click the **ChartWizard** tool and the mouse pointer changes to **+**.

Chart Type (Step 2 of 5)

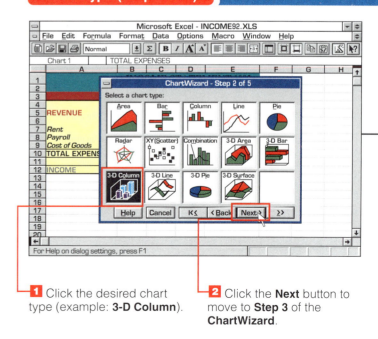

1 Click the desired chart type (example: **3-D Column**).

2 Click the **Next** button to move to **Step 3** of the **ChartWizard**.

| CREATE A CHART | MOVE A CHART | RESIZE A CHART | CHANGE CHART DATA | CHANGE CHART TYPE OR FORMAT | ROTATE A CHART |

5 Move the mouse pointer + to the position where you want to locate the top left corner of the chart.

6 Click and hold down the left mouse button as you drag to form a rectangular area to place the chart.

7 Release the mouse button and the **ChartWizard** dialog box appears, displaying the range of cells you wish to chart.

8 Click the **Next** button to move to **Step 2** of the **ChartWizard**.

Chart Format (Step 3 of 5)

1 Click the desired chart format (example: **4**).

2 Click the **Next** button to move to **Step 4** of the **ChartWizard**.

Note: For details on Steps **4** and **5** of the **ChartWizard**, refer to page 68.

CHARTWIZARD BUTTONS

Button	Description
Help	Click this button to display help information.
Cancel	Click this button to cancel the creation of the chart.
|<<	Click this button to return to the first step of the ChartWizard.
< Back	Click this button to return to the previous step.
Next >	Click this button to go to the next step.
>>	Click this button to finish the chart using the choices you have made so far.

GETTING STARTED

ENTER DATA

ENTER FORMULAS AND FUNCTIONS

MANAGING YOUR FILES

EDIT A WORKSHEET

FORMAT A WORKSHEET

CREATE AND EDIT A CHART

PRINT

OUTLINE A WORKSHEET

CREATE AND USE A DATABASE

67

CREATE A CHART

Plot Data by Rows or by Columns (Step 4 of 5)

- A sample of your chart is displayed.

- Each row you selected on your worksheet to produce this chart is displayed as a different colored bar (example: **REVENUE** is red).

1 To make the colored bars represent the columns of data from your worksheet, instead of the rows, click the circle beside **Columns** and ○ becomes ⦿.

- The colored bars now represent the columns of data from your worksheet.

2 To make the colored bars represent the rows of data from your worksheet (as before), click the circle beside **Rows** and ○ becomes ⦿.

3 Click the **Next** button to move to **Step 5** of the **ChartWizard**.

Chart Titles and Legend (Step 5 of 5)

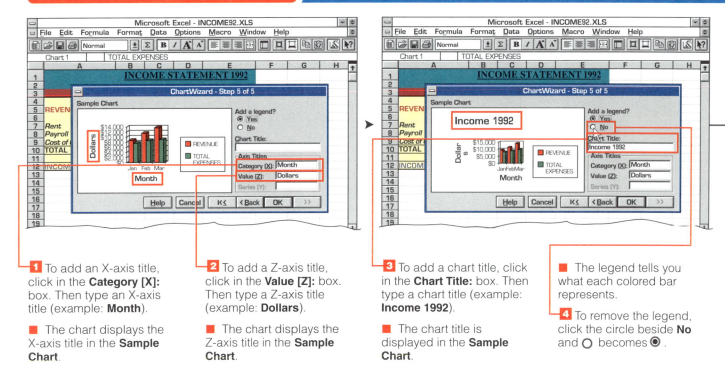

1 To add an X-axis title, click in the **Category [X]:** box. Then type an X-axis title (example: **Month**).

- The chart displays the X-axis title in the **Sample Chart**.

2 To add a Z-axis title, click in the **Value [Z]:** box. Then type a Z-axis title (example: **Dollars**).

- The chart displays the Z-axis title in the **Sample Chart**.

3 To add a chart title, click in the **Chart Title:** box. Then type a chart title (example: **Income 1992**).

- The chart title is displayed in the **Sample Chart**.

- The legend tells you what each colored bar represents.

4 To remove the legend, click the circle beside **No** and ○ becomes ⦿.

| CREATE A CHART | MOVE A CHART | RESIZE A CHART | CHANGE CHART DATA | CHANGE CHART TYPE OR FORMAT | ROTATE A CHART |

IMPORTANT

- The chart is linked to the data. This means that if you later make changes to the worksheet data, the chart automatically displays those changes.

- When you save the worksheet, the chart is saved with it.

- The legend is removed from the chart.

5 To add the legend (as before), click the circle beside **Yes** and ○ becomes ◉.

6 Click the **OK** button to view the chart on your worksheet.

- The chart appears.

Note: In this example, the chart is too large to be fully displayed in the given space. To change the size of the chart, refer to 'Resize a Chart' on page 71.

7 The **Chart** toolbar is displayed. If this toolbar hides part of your chart or worksheet, move it to a new position by dragging its title bar.

GETTING STARTED

ENTER DATA

ENTER FORMULAS AND FUNCTIONS

MANAGING YOUR FILES

EDIT A WORKSHEET

FORMAT A WORKSHEET

CREATE AND EDIT A CHART

PRINT

OUTLINE A WORKSHEET

CREATE AND USE A DATABASE

69

MOVE A CHART   RESIZE A CHART   CHANGE CHART DATA

Move a Chart

1 To select a chart to be moved, click anywhere inside the chart. Black squares ■ appear around its edges.

2 Click the left mouse button and hold it down as you drag the chart to a new position.

3 Release the mouse button and the chart is moved.

Change Chart Data

   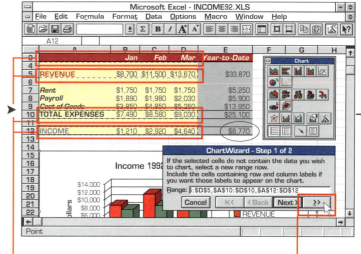

Data from your worksheet can be added to a chart by using the ChartWizard.

1 To select the chart you want to add data to, click anywhere inside the chart.

2 Click the **ChartWizard** tool and the **ChartWizard** dialog box appears.

3 If the **ChartWizard** hides part of your worksheet, move it to a new position by dragging the **ChartWizard** title bar.

4 Select the column headings you want to chart (example: **A3** to **D3**).

5 Press and hold down the **Ctrl** key as you select the other rows you want to chart (example: **A5** to **D5**, then **A10** to **D10**, then **A12** to **D12**).

6 Release the mouse button, then the **Ctrl** key.

7 Click the ⟫ button.

| CREATE A CHART | MOVE A CHART | RESIZE A CHART | CHANGE CHART DATA | CHANGE CHART TYPE OR FORMAT | ROTATE A CHART |

Resize a Chart

1 To select a chart to be resized, click anywhere inside the chart.

2 Move the mouse pointer over the bottom left corner of the chart box and it changes to ↙.

3 Click and hold down the left mouse button as you drag the corner of the chart to the desired size.

Note: You can drag any corner of the chart to resize it in different ways.

4 Release the mouse button and the chart is resized.

DELETE A CHART

1 Click anywhere inside the chart to select it.

2 Press the **Delete** key.

*Note: To immediately undo the deletion, click **Edit** to open its menu. Then click **Undo Clear**.*

8 Click the **down** scroll arrow to view more of the chart.

■ The new data (example: **INCOME** values) is plotted.

GETTING STARTED

ENTER DATA

ENTER FORMULAS AND FUNCTIONS

MANAGING YOUR FILES

EDIT A WORKSHEET

FORMAT A WORKSHEET

CREATE AND EDIT A CHART

PRINT

OUTLINE A WORKSHEET

CREATE AND USE A DATABASE

71

CHANGE CHART TYPE OR FORMAT

Change Chart Type or Format Using the Chart Gallery

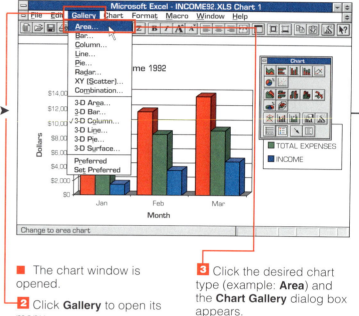

1 Double click anywhere inside the chart to open the chart window.

■ The chart window is opened.

2 Click **Gallery** to open its menu.

3 Click the desired chart type (example: **Area**) and the **Chart Gallery** dialog box appears.

Change Chart Type or Format Using the Chart Tools

The Charting toolbar offers the most popular formats for each chart type.

1 Click the tool that represents the chart type and format you want to change to (example: ▦).

Note: If the **Chart** toolbar is not displayed on the screen, it may be hidden. To display the toolbar, refer to page 52.

■ The new chart type and format are displayed (example: **3-D Bar Chart**).

2 Click another tool that represents the chart type and format you want to change to (example: ▦).

72

CREATE A CHART | MOVE A CHART | RESIZE A CHART | CHANGE CHART DATA | **CHANGE CHART TYPE OR FORMAT** | ROTATE A CHART

4 Click the desired chart format (example: **1**).

Note: Click [Next...] to view the next chart type in the **Chart Gallery**.

Click [Previous...] to view the previous chart type in the **Chart Gallery**.

5 Click the **OK** button.

■ The new chart type and format are displayed (example: **Simple Area Chart**).

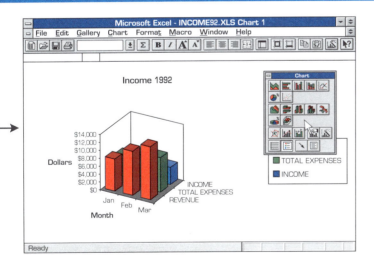

■ The new chart type and format are displayed (example: **3-D Perspective Column Chart**).

You can instantly change the chart type or format by clicking any one of these chart tools.

GETTING STARTED

ENTER DATA

ENTER FORMULAS AND FUNCTIONS

MANAGING YOUR FILES

EDIT A WORKSHEET

FORMAT A WORKSHEET

CREATE AND EDIT A CHART

PRINT

OUTLINE A WORKSHEET

CREATE AND USE A DATABASE

73

ROTATE A CHART

Rotate a Chart Using the Mouse

1 Click one of the corners of the chart and black squares ■ appear at each corner of the 3-D chart.

Note: You can only rotate three-dimensional charts.

2 Move the mouse pointer over one of these black squares ■.

3 Click the left mouse button and hold it down as you drag the square, rotating the chart to the desired rotation.

*Note: To view an outline of the chart as you rotate the chart, press and hold down the **Ctrl** key before proceeding with step 3.*

Rotate a Chart Using the 3-D View Command

1 Click **Format** to open its menu.

2 Click **3-D View** and its dialog box appears.

3 To change the **Elevation**, **Perspective**, or **Rotation** of the chart, click the desired buttons.

4 Click the **Default** button to return to the original rotation setting.

5 Click the **OK** button.

| CREATE A CHART | MOVE A CHART | RESIZE A CHART | CHANGE CHART DATA | CHANGE CHART TYPE OR FORMAT | **ROTATE A CHART** |

4 Release the mouse button and the rotation is complete.

Note: You can rotate the chart as many times as desired.

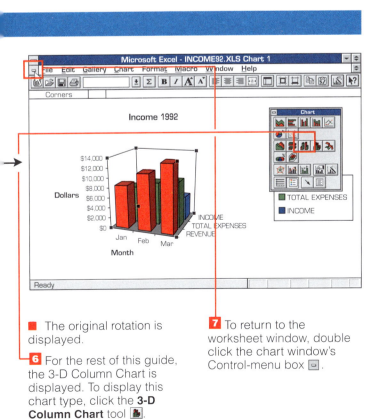

■ The original rotation is displayed.

6 For the rest of this guide, the 3-D Column Chart is displayed. To display this chart type, click the **3-D Column Chart** tool.

7 To return to the worksheet window, double click the chart window's Control-menu box.

 ADD OR REMOVE A LEGEND

1 Click anywhere inside the chart to select it.

2 Click the **Legend** tool.

*Note: To add the legend, click the **Legend** tool again.*

 ADD OR REMOVE GRIDLINES

1 Click anywhere inside the chart to select it.

2 Click the **Horizontal Gridlines** tool.

*Note: To remove the gridlines, click the **Horizontal Gridlines** tool again.*

GETTING STARTED

ENTER DATA

ENTER FORMULAS AND FUNCTIONS

MANAGING YOUR FILES

EDIT A WORKSHEET

FORMAT A WORKSHEET

CREATE AND EDIT A CHART

PRINT

OUTLINE A WORKSHEET

CREATE AND USE A DATABASE

75

CHANGE PAGE SETUP

Display the Page Setup Dialog Box

Page Setup changes can be made by using the Page Setup dialog box.

1 Click **File** to open its menu.

2 Click **Page Setup**.

■ The **Page Setup** dialog box appears.

Change Margins

1 Double click in any box under the **Margins** heading that you want to change (example: **Top**).

2 Type the new margin (example: **3**). This is defined in inches.

3 To center the page vertically, click the square beside **Vertically** and ☐ becomes ☒.

4 To center the page horizontally, click the square beside **Horizontally** and ☐ becomes ☒.

You can change the **Left**, **Right**, **Top** and **Bottom** margins.

Note: Margins define the distance between the printed worksheet and the edge of the paper.

You can **Vertically** and/or **Horizontally** center data on the printed page.

| CHANGE PAGE SETUP | PREVIEW A WORKSHEET | PRINT A WORKSHEET |

Print Worksheet Headings, Gridlines and Color

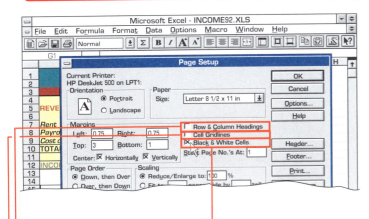

1 To print row and column headings, click the box beside **Row & Column Headings** and ☐ becomes ☒.

Note: In this example, the row and column headings will not be printed.

2 If you do not want to print the gridlines, click the box beside **Cell Gridlines** and ☒ becomes ☐.

3 To print the document in black and white, click the box beside **Black & White Cells** and ☐ becomes ☒.

Note: If a colored worksheet is printed on a black and white printer, it may be difficult to read the printed text. To solve this problem, print the document in black and white.

Change Page Orientation and Starting Page Number

The **Portrait** orientation prints the worksheet down the length of the paper.

The **Landscape** orientation prints the worksheet across the width of the paper.

■ The default setting is the **Portrait** orientation.

1 To change the orientation to **Landscape**, click **Landscape** and ○ becomes ◉.

*Note: In this example, the worksheet will be printed using the **Portrait** orientation.*

2 To change the number you want the page numbering to start with, double click in the box beside **Start Page No.'s At:**. Then type the number.

3 Click the **OK** button to return to the worksheet.

GETTING STARTED

ENTER DATA

ENTER FORMULAS AND FUNCTIONS

MANAGING YOUR FILES

EDIT A WORKSHEET

FORMAT A WORKSHEET

CREATE AND EDIT A CHART

PRINT

OUTLINE A WORKSHEET

CREATE AND USE A DATABASE

77

PREVIEW A WORKSHEET

Preview a Worksheet Before Printing

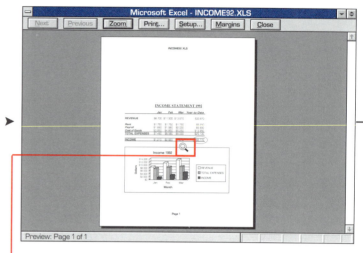

You can see how the worksheet will look on a printed page before you actually print it.

1 Click **File** to open its menu.

2 Click **Print Preview**.

3 Move the mouse pointer over the area of the worksheet you want to view up close and it changes to 🔍 (magnifying glass). Click the left mouse button.

Margins — Change Margins or Column Widths

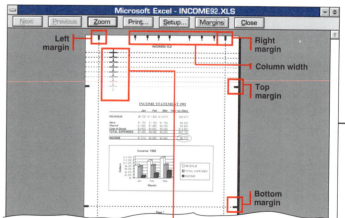

1 To display the current margins and column width settings, click the **Margins** button.

Note: You can also change margins by using the Page Setup dialog box. For more information, refer to page 76.

■ The current margins and column width settings are displayed.

2 Move the mouse pointer over the margin or column width setting you want to change and 🔍 becomes ↕ or ↔. Click and hold down the left mouse button.

3 Still holding down the button, drag the margin or column width to a new position.

CHANGE
PAGE SETUP

**PREVIEW A
WORKSHEET**

PRINT A
WORKSHEET

■ The area is viewed at its actual printed size.

4 Click the **up** or **down arrows** to scroll vertically through the page.

5 Click the **left** or **right arrows** to scroll horizontally through the page.

6 To return to the full-page view, click anywhere on the worksheet.

Click this button to view the next page in the document.

Click this button to view the previous page in the document.

Click this button to view the **Print** dialog box.

Click this button to view the **Page Setup** dialog box.

Click this button to close the Print Preview window.

*Note: The **Next** and **Previous** buttons appear dimmed if the document contains only one page.*

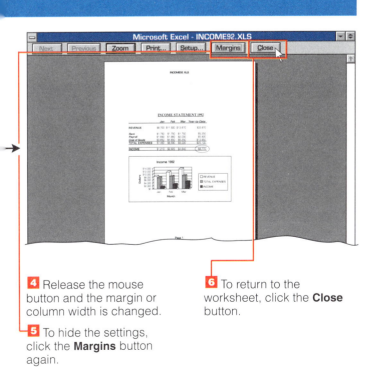

4 Release the mouse button and the margin or column width is changed.

5 To hide the settings, click the **Margins** button again.

6 To return to the worksheet, click the **Close** button.

GETTING
STARTED

●

ENTER
DATA

●

ENTER
FORMULAS
AND FUNCTIONS

●

MANAGING
YOUR
FILES

●

EDIT A
WORKSHEET

●

FORMAT A
WORKSHEET

●

CREATE AND
EDIT A CHART

PRINT

●

OUTLINE A
WORKSHEET

●

CREATE AND
USE A
DATABASE

79

PRINT A WORKSHEET

Print a Worksheet

1 Click **File** to open its menu.

2 Click **Print** and the **Print** dialog box appears.

Note: To only print a chart, the chart must be displayed in a chart window. To open a chart window, double click anywhere inside the chart.

Print Quality

■ As the print quality decreases, the printer produces a faster, lower quality image.

3 Click the arrow ⬇ beside the **Print Quality:** box and the print quality options for your printer are displayed.

4 Click the desired print quality (example: **300 dpi**).

Note: Other printers may have different print quality options.

Number of Copies

■ The default setting is **1** copy.

5 To print multiple copies, double click in the **Copies:** box. Then type the number of copies you want to print.

 PRINT USING THE PRINT TOOL

To quickly print your worksheet using the current settings, click the **Print** tool.

CHANGE PAGE SETUP   PREVIEW A WORKSHEET   **PRINT A WORKSHEET**

Print Range

■ **All** is the default setting. All pages in the worksheet will be printed.

6 To print specific pages instead of all pages, click in the **From:** box. Then type the starting page number.

7 Click in the **To:** box and type the last page number.

8 Click the **OK** button, or press **Enter**.

■ The worksheet is printed.

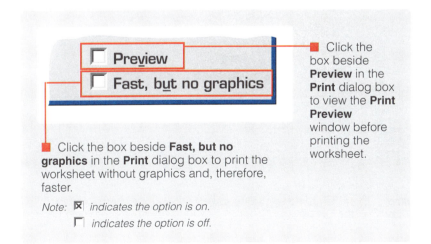

■ Click the box beside **Preview** in the **Print** dialog box to view the **Print Preview** window before printing the worksheet.

■ Click the box beside **Fast, but no graphics** in the **Print** dialog box to print the worksheet without graphics and, therefore, faster.

Note: ☒ indicates the option is on.
☐ indicates the option is off.

GETTING STARTED

ENTER DATA

ENTER FORMULAS AND FUNCTIONS

MANAGING YOUR FILES

EDIT A WORKSHEET

FORMAT A WORKSHEET

CREATE AND EDIT A CHART

PRINT

OUTLINE A WORKSHEET

CREATE AND USE A DATABASE

81

DISPLAY THE UTILITY TOOLBAR

CREATE AN OUTLINE

OUTLINE A WORKSHEET

Before Outline

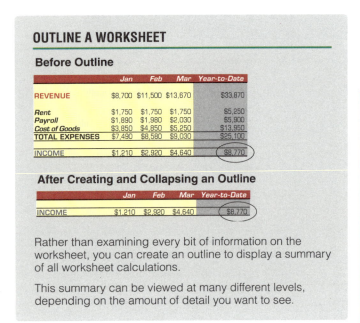

After Creating and Collapsing an Outline

Rather than examining every bit of information on the worksheet, you can create an outline to display a summary of all worksheet calculations.

This summary can be viewed at many different levels, depending on the amount of detail you want to see.

Display the Utility Toolbar

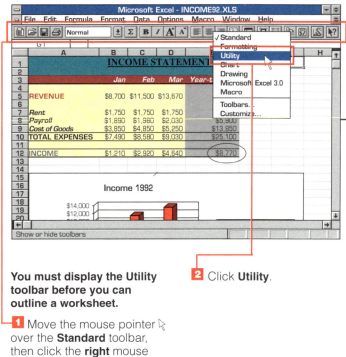

You must display the Utility toolbar before you can outline a worksheet.

1 Move the mouse pointer over the **Standard** toolbar, then click the **right** mouse button.

2 Click **Utility**.

 Create an Outline

1 Select the cells that contain the data you want to outline.

2 Click the **Show Outline Symbols** tool on the **Utility** toolbar.

3 To create an outline, click the **OK** button.

Note: This dialog box only appears if no previous outline was created for the worksheet.

| DISPLAY THE UTILITY TOOLBAR | CREATE AN OUTLINE | COLLAPSE A LEVEL | EXPAND A LEVEL | HIDE AN OUTLINE |

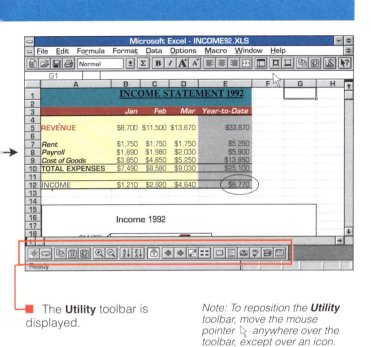

■ The **Utility** toolbar is displayed.

Note: To reposition the **Utility** toolbar, move the mouse pointer anywhere over the toolbar, except over an icon. Click and hold down the left mouse button as you drag the toolbar to the new position.

■ The outline symbols are displayed.

4 To deselect a range of cells, click any cell in the worksheet (example: **G1**).

■ This symbol indicates that the data in the rows beside it (example: **Rent**, **Payroll**, **Cost of Goods**) were calculated together to determine the values beside the ■ symbol (example: **Total Expenses**).

■ This symbol indicates that the data in the columns under it (example: **Jan**, **Feb**, **Mar**) were calculated together to determine the values under the ■ symbol (example: **Year-to-Date**).

GETTING STARTED

ENTER DATA

ENTER FORMULAS AND FUNCTIONS

MANAGING YOUR FILES

EDIT A WORKSHEET

FORMAT A WORKSHEET

CREATE AND EDIT A CHART

PRINT

OUTLINE A WORKSHEET

CREATE AND USE A DATABASE

83

COLLAPSE A LEVEL   EXPAND A LEVEL   HIDE AN OUTLINE

Collapse a Level

You can hide data by collapsing rows and columns. This makes it easier to view important data in your worksheet.

1 To hide the data used to calculate the values beside the ➖ symbol, click that Collapse symbol ➖.

■ The data is hidden (example: **Rent**, **Payroll** and **Cost of Goods**).

2 Click another Collapse symbol ➖ for the data you want to hide.

Expand a Level

You can display hidden data by expanding rows and columns.

1 To display the data used to calculate the values beside the ➕ symbol, click that Expand symbol ➕.

■ The data is displayed (example: **Revenue** and **Total Expenses**).

2 Click another Expand symbol ➕ for the data you want to display.

DISPLAY THE UTILITY TOOLBAR | CREATE AN OUTLINE | **COLLAPSE A LEVEL** | **EXPAND A LEVEL** | **HIDE AN OUTLINE**

You can also collapse and expand data by clicking one of these symbols.

Click this symbol to display the data for 1 level of information.

Click this symbol to display the data for 2 levels of information.

Click this symbol to display the data for 3 levels of information.

Note: A worksheet can contain up to 8 levels of information.

■ The data is hidden (example: **Revenue** and **Total Expenses**).

Note: You can collapse rows and columns.

Hide an Outline

■ The data is displayed (example: **Rent**, **Payroll** and **Cost of Goods**).

1 To hide the outline, click the **Show Outline Symbols** tool.

*Note: To display the outline, click the **Show Outline Symbols** tool again.*

GETTING STARTED

ENTER DATA

ENTER FORMULAS AND FUNCTIONS

MANAGING YOUR FILES

EDIT A WORKSHEET

FORMAT A WORKSHEET

CREATE AND EDIT A CHART

PRINT

OUTLINE A WORKSHEET

CREATE AND USE A DATABASE

85

CREATE A DATABASE   SORT A DATABASE

Create a Database

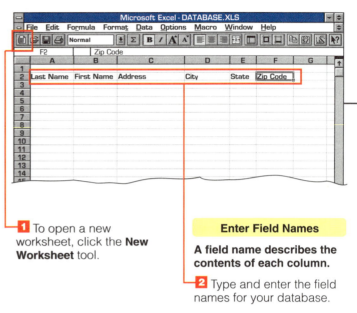

■ A database is a collection of related data in rows and columns in a worksheet. It consists of field names (identifies the information in each column) and records (rows of data). Typical databases include library card catalogs, accounts receivable information, mailing lists, and telephone lists.

■ A database can be created using the same skills you have learned in Microsoft Excel for creating a worksheet.

■ A database is used to organize, manage, sort and retrieve information from large and complex collections of data.

1 To open a new worksheet, click the **New Worksheet** tool.

Enter Field Names

A field name describes the contents of each column.

2 Type and enter the field names for your database.

Sort a Database

1 Select the cells that contain the data you want to sort.

Note: Do not select the field names, otherwise they will be sorted with the data.

2 Click **Data** to open its menu.

3 Click **Sort**.

Note: Before sorting the database, you may want to save it to retain the presorted order of the data. To save a worksheet, refer to page 34.

4 Select any cell (example: **A5**) in the column you want to base the sort on. This is called the **1st Key**.

*Note: If the **Sort** dialog box covers the database, move the box by dragging its title bar.*

5 Click the circle beside the desired sort order (example: **Ascending**) and ○ becomes ⦿.

Note: Ascending sorts data A through Z, and 0-9. Descending sorts data Z through A, and 9-0.

| CREATE A DATABASE | SORT A DATABASE | DISPLAY THE DATA FORM | ADD A RECORD | FIND A RECORD | CHANGE A RECORD | DELETE A RECORD | EXTRACT RECORDS |

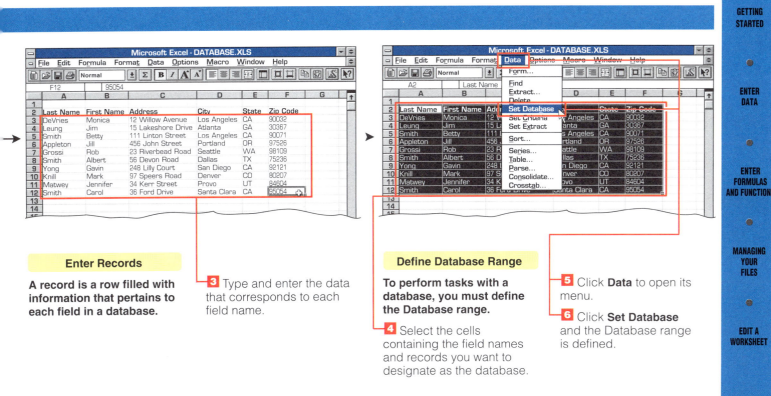

Enter Records

A record is a row filled with information that pertains to each field in a database.

3 Type and enter the data that corresponds to each field name.

Define Database Range

To perform tasks with a database, you must define the Database range.

4 Select the cells containing the field names and records you want to designate as the database.

5 Click **Data** to open its menu.

6 Click **Set Database** and the Database range is defined.

6 If Microsoft Excel finds matching entries in the 1st key (example: the last name **Smith**), the 2nd key option can be specified to serve as a "tie-breaker". Click in the box under **2nd Key**.

7 Select any cell (example: **B5**) in the column you want to serve as a "tie-breaker".

8 Click the circle beside the desired sort order (example: **Ascending**) and ○ becomes ⦿.

9 Click the **OK** button, or press **Enter**.

■ The Last Names are sorted in ascending order.

■ The Last Name **Smith** appears three times. The 2nd key option then sorts the First Names in ascending order (example: **Albert**, **Betty** and **Carol**).

Note: To deselect cells, click anywhere on the worksheet.

GETTING STARTED

ENTER DATA

ENTER FORMULAS AND FUNCTIONS

MANAGING YOUR FILES

EDIT A WORKSHEET

FORMAT A WORKSHEET

CREATE AND EDIT A CHART

PRINT

OUTLINE A WORKSHEET

CREATE AND USE A DATABASE

DISPLAY THE DATA FORM   ADD A RECORD   FIND A RECORD

Display the Data Form

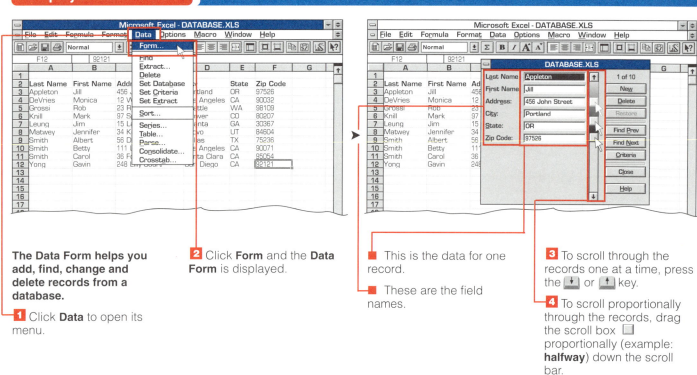

The Data Form helps you add, find, change and delete records from a database.

1 Click **Data** to open its menu.

2 Click **Form** and the **Data Form** is displayed.

■ This is the data for one record.

■ These are the field names.

3 To scroll through the records one at a time, press the ↓ or ↑ key.

4 To scroll proportionally through the records, drag the scroll box ☐ proportionally (example: **halfway**) down the scroll bar.

Find a Record

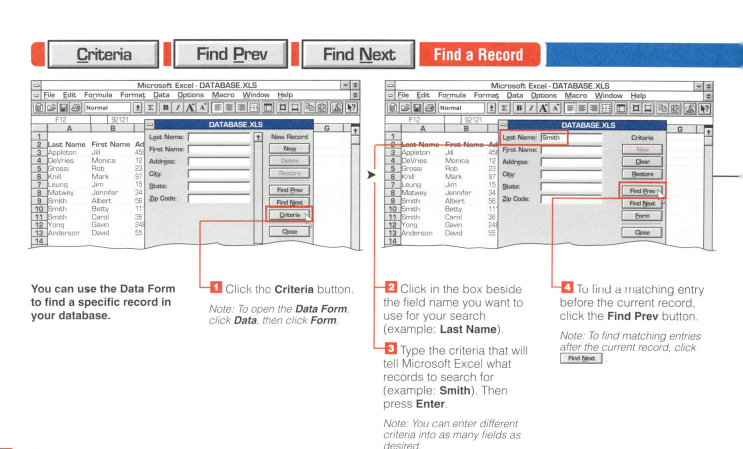

You can use the Data Form to find a specific record in your database.

1 Click the **Criteria** button.

Note: To open the **Data Form**, click **Data**, then click **Form**.

2 Click in the box beside the field name you want to use for your search (example: **Last Name**).

3 Type the criteria that will tell Microsoft Excel what records to search for (example: **Smith**). Then press **Enter**.

Note: You can enter different criteria into as many fields as desired.

4 To find a matching entry before the current record, click the **Find Prev** button.

Note: To find matching entries after the current record, click Find Next.

| CREATE A DATABASE | SORT A DATABASE | DISPLAY THE DATA FORM | ADD A RECORD | FIND A RECORD | CHANGE A RECORD | DELETE A RECORD | EXTRACT RECORDS |

Add a Record

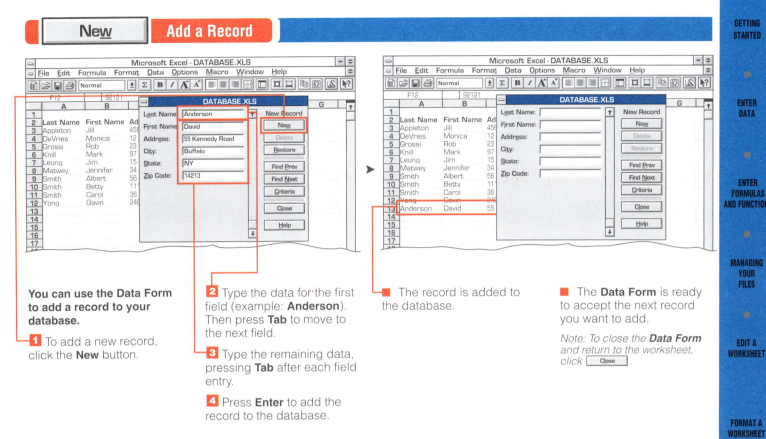

You can use the Data Form to add a record to your database.

1 To add a new record, click the **New** button.

2 Type the data for the first field (example: **Anderson**). Then press **Tab** to move to the next field.

3 Type the remaining data, pressing **Tab** after each field entry.

4 Press **Enter** to add the record to the database.

■ The record is added to the database.

■ The **Data Form** is ready to accept the next record you want to add.

Note: To close the Data Form and return to the worksheet, click [Close].

■ A record that matches the criteria is displayed.

5 To find another matching entry before the current record, click the **Find Prev** button again.

Note: The computer beeps when it cannot find another matching entry.

DEFINING THE CRITERIA

Operator	Examples:	
=	=10	finds all entries equal to 10
>	>10	finds all entries greater than 10
<	<10	finds all entries less than 10
>=	>=10	finds all entries greater than and equal to 10
<=	<=10	finds all entries less than and equal to 10
<>	<>10	finds all entries not equal to 10

Note: These operators can also be used with text.

Wildcard Characters

* When you use an ***** (asterisk) in a criterion, the ***** is interpreted to mean any number of characters (example: **Jo*** finds all entries starting with Jo).

? When you use a **?** (question mark) in a criterion, the **?** is interpreted to mean any character in that position (example: **Jo?n** finds Joan and John).

GETTING STARTED

ENTER DATA

ENTER FORMULAS AND FUNCTIONS

MANAGING YOUR FILES

EDIT A WORKSHEET

FORMAT A WORKSHEET

CREATE AND EDIT A CHART

PRINT

OUTLINE A WORKSHEET

CREATE AND USE A DATABASE

CHANGE A RECORD

DELETE A RECORD

Change a Record

You can use the Data Form to change a record in your database.

1 Use the scroll bar, or press the ↓ or ↑ key until the record you want to change appears.

Note: To open the Data Form, click Data, then click Form.

To quickly display a record you want to change, use the Find function. For more information, refer to page 88.

2 Press **Tab** until the information you want to change is highlighted (example: **First Name**).

Delete a Record

You can use the Data Form to delete a record from your database.

1 Use the scroll bar or press the ↓ or ↑ key to view the record you want to delete.

Note: To quickly display a record you want to delete, use the Find function. For more information, refer to page 88.

2 Click the **Delete** button.

■ A dialog box appears to confirm the deletion.

3 Click the **OK** button to delete the record.

CREATE A DATABASE SORT A DATABASE DISPLAY THE DATA FORM ADD A RECORD FIND A RECORD **CHANGE A RECORD** **DELETE A RECORD** EXTRACT RECORDS

3 Type the correction (example: **Justin**).

4 Press **Enter**, and the change is made to the database.

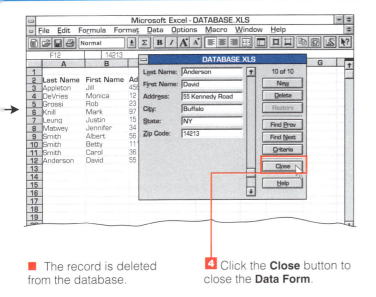

■ The record is deleted from the database.

4 Click the **Close** button to close the **Data Form**.

GETTING STARTED

ENTER DATA

ENTER FORMULAS AND FUNCTIONS

MANAGING YOUR FILES

EDIT A WORKSHEET

FORMAT A WORKSHEET

CREATE AND EDIT A CHART

PRINT

OUTLINE A WORKSHEET

CREATE AND USE A DATABASE

91

EXTRACT RECORDS

Copy Field Names

1 Before extracting data, you must copy the field names to two different areas on the worksheet.

Note: To copy data, refer to page 48.

Define Criteria and Criteria Range

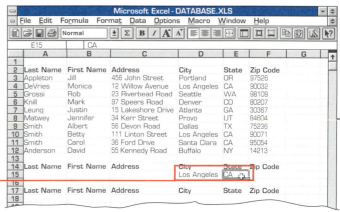

The criteria tells Microsoft Excel what data to search for.

1 Decide what information you want to extract from the database. Then, under the appropriate heading(s), type and enter your criteria.

Note: The criteria in this example will extract all records of persons living in Los Angeles, CA.

Extract Records

Extracting records involves searching the database for specific records that match the criteria set above.

1 Select the cells that contain the field names where you want to copy the extracted data.

2 Click **Data** to open its menu.

3 Click **Extract**, and the **Extract** dialog box appears.

4 Click the **OK** button.

*Note: If you click the box beside **Unique Records Only**, only one copy of each repeated record will be extracted.*

CREATE A DATABASE   SORT A DATABASE   DISPLAY THE DATA FORM   ADD A RECORD   FIND A RECORD   CHANGE A RECORD   DELETE A RECORD   **EXTRACT RECORDS**

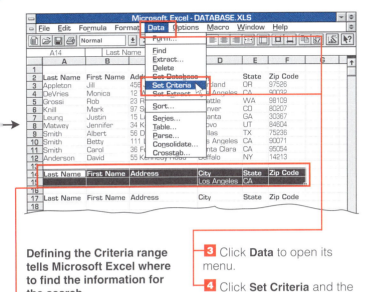

Defining the Criteria range tells Microsoft Excel where to find the information for the search.

2 Select the cells containing the field names and the criteria you want to designate as the data needed for the search.

3 Click **Data** to open its menu.

4 Click **Set Criteria** and the Criteria range is defined.

DEFINING THE CRITERIA

Operator	Examples:	
=	=10	finds all entries equal to 10
>	>10	finds all entries greater than 10
<	<10	finds all entries less than 10
>=	>=10	finds all entries greater than and equal to 10
<=	<=10	finds all entries less than and equal to 10
<>	<>10	finds all entries not equal to 10

Note: These operators can also be used with text.

Wildcard Characters

*	When you use an ***** (asterisk) in a criterion, the ***** is interpreted to mean any number of characters (example: **Jo*** finds all entries starting with Jo).
?	When you use a **?** (question mark) in a criterion, the **?** is interpreted to mean any character in that position (example: **Jo?n** finds Joan and John).

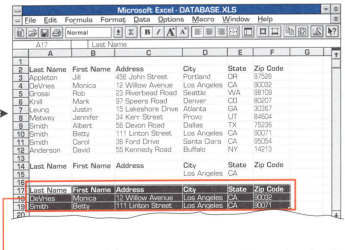

■ The requested data satisfying your criteria is copied to the new location.

Note: This data can be printed and analyzed.

93

INDEX

CHART
Change Data 70
Change Type or Format..................72
Create 66-68
Delete 71
Move 70
Resize 71
Rotate 74

COLUMN
Delete 47
Insert 47
Width...............................42, 43, 78

DATABASE
Add a Record 89
Change a Record 90
Create 86
Delete a Record..............................90
Display the Data Form 88
Extract Records 92
Find a Record 88
Sort 86

DELETE
Chart 71
Column 47
Data 20
Object 65
Row 46
Worksheet 40

DRAW
Color 65
Lines 64
Shapes..64

FILE SPECIFICATION 32

FORMATS
AutoFormat 62
Bold 60
Borders 58
Copy and Paste 60
Italic 60
Remove 59
Shading 58
Strikeout 61
Underline 61

FORMULAS
Absolute References 30
AutoFill...24
Automatic Recalculation 25
Enter...24
Introduction 22
Order of Precedence 22

FUNCTIONS
Absolute References 30
Arguments 27
AutoFill...30
Enter...28
Introduction 26
Sum Using the AutoSum Tool 28

HELP
Contents 8
Context Sensitive..............................8

MICROSOFT EXCEL
Exit...6
Start..4

MOVE THROUGH A WORKSHEET
Using the Keyboard 12
Using the Mouse 13

NUMBERS
AutoFill.....................................18, 20
Copy 48, 50
Delete 20
Edit 16
Enter...14
Fonts 54
Format..52
Left, Center, Right Align 56
Long 15
Move 48, 50

OUTLINE
Collapse a Level..............................84
Create..82
Expand a Level 84
Hide..85

PRINT
Change Page Setup 76, 77
Preview...78
Print 80

ROW
Delete 46
Height 44, 45
Insert..46

SAVE
Changes 7, 37
New Worksheet...............................34
Revised Worksheet.........................35
To a Different Drive........................36

SELECT
Cell...10
Cell Range 10
Column 11
Entire Worksheet.............................11
Row 10
Two Cell Ranges..............................11

TEXT
AutoFill...18
Center Across Selected Columns ...56
Copy 48, 50
Delete 20
Edit...16
Enter...14
Fonts 54
Justify...57
Left, Center, Right Align 56
Long 15
Move 48, 50

TOOLBAR
Display or Hide 52
Drawing 64
Formatting.......................................52
Utility 82

UNDO 16

WORKSHEET
Arrange 40
Close..36
Create 38
Delete 40
Maximize...6
Open 38
Print..80
Restore 6
Save...34-36
Switch Between 39